Hip-Hop Homophobes

Other books by Khalil Amani:

Ghetto Religiosity 2000: Third Millennium Liberation.

Ghetto Religiosity II: Uncovering The Naked Truth.

Ghetto Religiosity III: If You Don't Know,
Now You Know!

Hip-Hop-perations: surgical essays and poems for the ghetto mind.

My id ... Ignant & Dissfunkshunal! Life in the Yahweh Cult and the Witness Protection Program.

Orderable at www.iuniverse.com, Barnes and Noble, Amazon.com, Borders and many other bookstores.

Visit @ www.myspace.com/khalilamani
Email: khalilamani@yahoo.com

Hip-Hop Homophobes

✦

Origin & Attitudes Towards
Gays & Lesbians in Hip Hop Culture;
As Perpetuated by
Rappers, Thugs, Athletes, Reggae Rastas
& Religionists;
Essays on the 3,000 Year Old Polemic
Against Homosexuality; A Religious
Hoax!

Khalil Amani, S.A.
A Hip-Hopper's Spiritual Primer for
Overcoming Homophobia.

iUniverse, Inc.
New York Lincoln Shanghai

Hip-Hop Homophobes
Origin & Attitudes Towards
Gays & Lesbians in Hip Hop Culture;
As Perpetuated byRappers, Thugs, Athletes, Reggae Rastas & Religionists;
Essays on the 3,000 Year Old Polemic Against Homosexuality; A Religious Hoax!

iUniverse books may be ordered through booksellers or by contacting:

iUniverse
2021 Pine Lake Road, Suite 100
Lincoln, NE 68512
www.iuniverse.com
1-800-Authors (1-800-288-4677)

Because of the dynamic nature of the Internet, any Web addresses or links contained in this book may have changed since publication and may no longer be valid.

The views expressed in this work are solely those of the author and do not necessarily reflect the views of the publisher, and the publisher hereby disclaims any responsibility for them.

ISBN: 978-0-595-47541-4 (pbk)
ISBN: 978-0-595-91810-2 (ebk)

Printed in the United States of America

"… and whosoever shall say to his brother, 'RACA' (FAGGOT), shall be in danger of the council …"

St. Matthew 5:22

—Jesus Christ—On Homosexuality.

To These Wonderful and Courageous Souls Who Contributed Their Work to this Project in an effort to bring Homo-Hop Consciousness to the World!

Cat-Eyez ("Ghetto Prince Charming" Thanks for your help.)

Veto Ali (God feels your pain. R.I.P. Roy/Stepdad)

JenRO (Gangstress! U ain't hard to look at girl!☺)

El-Don (Lyrically Powerful!)

Shorty Roc (Long on Talent!)

Pam Jones (West Coast Hell Raisa!)

(Bone) Intell

(A "Gay Rapper"—Not a rapper who "raps gay!")

White Lesbian Rapper (WLR)

(I love your honesty. You make me smile!☺)

Salvimex (Latino Heat!) Bigg Nugg (Da Bear!)

FELONi (Five Mic CD! I love your shyt!)

Mz. Fontaine (U.K.'s Finest!)

Diamon D.I.V.A.

(Hometown kid! Rep that MIA to the fullest!)

Ricoshade (Mic Killa) Delacruz (Thugstress)

Foxxjazell (Phenomenal Woman!)

soce—the elemental wizard (You got it goin' on white boy!☺ Nice to have met you.)

Milo Management and a special shout-out to

Deadlee—"Gayngsta" "Homo-thug" (Thanks for allowing me into your life and being your spiritual advisor—I'm honored!)

Viva la HomoRevolucion!
I got love for all of you! Khalil Amani, S.A.

Contents

Gay Slurs Original Meanings ...
Before They Were Bastardized!

Faggot: Bundle of burning sticks. Homosexuals where doused with fuel and used in place of sticks for burning supposed witches in England during Medieval Times. Yiddish; faygele- "little bird." Fag-contemptible woman "old bag." Fag-young English boy who serves upperclassmen boys in British schools with no implications of homosexuality.

Gay: Carefree, happy, showy, bright.

Lesbian: Greek-Poet woman named Sappho (610-580 BC) wrote poetry about attraction to women. She was from the Island of LESBOS.

Queer: German-Strange, unusual, odd, out of alignment. Ex. Queer sense of humor.

Homo: Latin—"same," "man."

Dyke-Bulldyke-Bull dagger: During the 1920's Harlem Renaissance, this term was used by several black writers. The origin of the word is probably from an abbreviation of "hermaphrodite," which came from the 19th century use of "Dyke," (meaning ditch) as a slang for a woman's vulva. "Bull" is an expression for "masculine" or "aggressive."

Current Bigotry 101 Please Fill in the Blanks

"I hate _____ people, so I let it be known. I don't like _____ people and I don't like to be around _____ people. I am _____! I don't like it. It shouldn't be in the United States!"

A. Black

B. White

C. Asian

D. Hispanic

E. Jewish

F. Gay

G. Straight

H. Vertically Challenged

I. Mentally Challenged

J. Handicapped

K. Christian

L. Islamic

M. Hip Hop

N. Athletic

O. Racist, Homophobic, Prejudiced,

P. Bigoted, Ignorant, Etcetera, etc., etc.

<u>Answer:</u> F

*"... I hate **gay** people, so I let it be known. I don't like **gay** people and I don't like to be around **gay** people. I am **homophobic**! I don't like it. It shouldn't be in the world or in the United States!"*

—Tim Hardaway
Five-Time NBA All-Star Basketball Player Feb. 2007

The Genesis: Finding Homo-Hop

o o o o o o o o o o o o o o o o o o o o o o o o o o o o o o o o

"I'd rather fuck with the truth, than make love to a lie!"

—Lesbian Rapper FELONi

The groundwork for this book was written over seven years ago in a tome I wrote called **Ghetto Religiosity II: Uncovering The Naked Truth** and another book I penned called **Hip-Hop-perations: surgical essays & poems for the ghetto mind** (iuniverse.com 2000, 2001). Two chapters I wrote back then are found within these pages: **"Homosexuality: The Great Sin of Sodom? Deconstructing The Biblical Myth Against Homosexuality"** and **"A Man Ain't Nothin' But A Homo!"**

Back then, I had no clue that there was something called "homo-hop." I didn't even know there were "gay" rappers. I was writing those chapters in support of gay/lesbian rights on some religious stuff, never intending to become a gay rights activist or represent a gay rap artist. I was simply exposing the fallacy of homophobia from a religious/biblical perspective, destroying the myth of a god's condemnation of a sexual/religious practice. My research revealed that anti-homosexual sentiments in the world were contrived in the name of a god to justify the religious practices of certain people.

Fast-forward seven years later (today). I'm reading an Internet blog about a gay gangsta rapper named Deadlee. I'm thinking "gay gangsta rapper?" *WTF?* Then I began to read the very ignorant and homophobic posts about this gay rapper. Downright mean-spirited! Hateration to the 10th power! I felt bad for the rapper, having to read all of this garbage. So I posted a positive comment and reached out to this gay rapper and let him know that there are some heterosexuals who feel your cause and to keep doing your thing. That's what true hip-hop is about—self-expression—keepin' it real—being true to who you are—do you!—and so forth and so on.

He responded back with a "thank you" and we began to email back and forth. I told him about my books and the chapter I'd written on homosexuality and how the Bible has misrepresented homosexuality as sin and to read it when he had a chance. He did. He gained some new spiritual insights and perspectives and I became his spiritual advisor. This is how I found homo-hop.

I didn't intend to become ingratiated in this genre of rap! It fell into my lap. After all that I'd written on homosexuality, I'd be a hypocrite to sit back and not let my voice be further heard for a worthy and just cause—homo-hop. Thus, this is what inspired me to write this book—***Hip-hop Homophobes*** ... *"To whom much is given, much is required." "When you know better, you do better!" "Ye shall know the truth, and the truth shall make you free." "To thine own self, be true."* These quotes have never been truer for me!

When I began to do the research on homophobia in hip-hop, I found many articles on the subject, but not ONE BOOK! I found books that dealt with the history of hip-hop, rap, B-Boys, break dancing, graffiti, scratching/Djing/turntablism, the greatest MC's, Tupac, misogyny, etc. But nobody addressed the blatant homophobia in hip-hop in a book! What a shame, I thought. So, as far as I'm aware, this is the FIRST BOOK written with the expressed intent and purpose of tearing down the walls of homophobia in hip-hop by exposing its origin and allowing the reader to see where their worldviews on homosexuality originated. This is also the FIRST BOOK to bring together homo rappers from around the country and the world—showing that gay and lesbian rap artists are a part of a larger genre of music—rap music! For that, I'm proud to be in the forefront of this movement to eradicate homophobia in the world, in general, and in the hip-hop community specifically.

Reppin' homo-hop as a straight man is revolutionary, in light of the homophobia in hip-hop. It is also eye-raising and the cause for speculation about one's sexuality—mine! But I'm not too concerned about that. I'm more concerned about the TRUTH! What is the truth? The truth is that homophobia is the result of a 3,000 year old religious pogrom that the world has bought—hook, line, and sinker!—A big-ass lie that we are forever cosigning in the name of our masculinity and heterosexuality. I don't care who your favorite rapper is and how much money they've got and how many records they sell—If they rap homophobic lyrics they are as ignorant and uninformed and brainwashed and indoctrinated and misinformed and culturally repressed as the day is long!

You see, I'm a real hip-hop head! I say "real" hip-hop head because a lot of y'all say you're hip-hop but then go on and try to define what "real" hip-hop is. All of it is REAL hip-hop—from the wackest MC you've ever heard to the dopest

MC you've ever heard! From the grimiest underground rapper to the most radio-friendly pop rapper! It's all hip-hop!

I'm **Ancient School** meets **Old School** meets **New School** meets **Homo School**! Ancient school? Yeah! Everybody wanna talk about those South Bronx rappers and the advent of rap/hip-hop with Afrika Bambaataa and Grandmaster Flash and them! But let me hip you young cats and catettes to ANCIENT SCHOOL RAP. I'm 47 years old. I go back to the original rappers—the progenitors of this rap shyt! Who am I talking about? THE LAST POETS! I was ten years old in 1970 when them niccas came out with *When The Revolution Comes, Niggers Are Scared of Revolution, Black Thighs,* etc. What you know 'bout dat? These brothas were rapping before many of you were born! Yeah, I here you! Rappers have this mentality that once you turn 30ish you should stop rapping, as though you have to be physically in shape like an athlete. Ever seen Fat Joe and Rick Ross? Got Jay-Z rapping, *"30 is the new 20."* Phuck that! Listen up all you young niccas! THE LAST POETS started all this rap shyt! Respect the architects! When you were an embryo in your mother's womb—while you were yet an unborn fetus—when you were a snotty-nosed bebe kid, these brothas were laying the foundation and groundwork for what would become known as "rap/hip-hop." So stop hatin' on the ancient and old school cats. 'Cause guess what? One day you will be an old school rapper to a younger generation! Just keep living. It is from their innovations in which you rappers eat. The word "rap" is not a new word, exclusive to the hip-hop generation! "Rap" has been a part of the 'hood-man's lexicon for many years. Ever heard of H Rap Brown—the activist? How about Jack "The Rapper" a.k.a. Joseph Gibson (R.I.P.), the pioneer of black radio? We used to lay a "rap game" on a girl in the '70s. Check out movies like *Superfly* and *The Mack* and many other '70s "Blaxploitation" movies and you will freely hear the word "rap" being used as an expression for talking or running game on a woman. *Can ya dig it baby?* The Last Poets were rappers in the purest form—without drum machines, 808s, synthesizers, sampling and heavy bass lines.

THE LAST POETS were poets, rappers, spoken-word artists and activists. If you claim to be hip-hop you need their album in your crate. I've got mine! And yes, the Last Poets were bitten by the cultural homophobia bug too when they rapped, *"When the revolution comes ... faggots won't be so funny then."*

Ever heard of Gil Scott-Heron? The next innovator of rap music. Gil Scott-Heron is considered by many as the "Godfather of Rap." In 1971 he dropped **Pieces of a Man.** His most famous song off that album, *The Revolution Will Not Be Televised* (1971) has been bitten by the likes of Elvis Costello, Public Enemy,

Prince, Common, KRS-One, Wu-Tang Clan, Bobby Brown, Cee-lo Green, Damian Marley, Jamiroquai and even *Apple* computers used Heron's famous social statement, *The Revolution Will Not Be Televised*. That's what rap is about—REVOLUTION! Go back and check your rap history pimpin'! THE LAST POETS, GIL SCOTT-HERON, THE WATTS POETS, Amiri Baraka (LeRoi Jones), Haki Madhubuti, Sonja Sanchez, Nikki Giovanni—these brothas and sistas were doin' it big back in the day! Out of that Movement birthed the likes of Afrika Bambaataa, DJ Kool Herc, Grandmaster Caz, Kurtis Blow and Sugar Hill Gang (the first nationally recognized rap group ca. 1979). They say "real recognize real." Rap music is not an island! Rap music follows one continuous vein that originated from the African Griot storytellers right on down to sista Sojourner Truth who rapped, *Ain't I A Woman?* to W.E.B. Dubois' *Talented Tenth* to Malcolm X's *The Ballot or the Bullet* to Martin Luther King's *I Have A Dream* to The Last Poets/Gil Scott-Heron's *When The Revolution Comes/ The Revolution Will Not Be Televised* to Rudy Ray Moore's (Dolemite) and Henry Louis Gate's *Signifying Monkey* to Richard Pryor's *Miss Rudolph* and *Mudbone* to Muhammad Ali's *I'm The Greatest* to Grandmaster Flash's *The Message* to Public Enemy's *Fight The Power* to Johnny Cochran's *If It Doesn't Fit, You Must Acquit!* to Nas' *I Know I can.* James Brown, Michael Jackson, Fab 5 Freddy, Savion Glover, MC Hammer, Tupac, Queen Latifah, Eminem, Deadlee, Nelson George, Toure, Kevin Powell, Saul Williams, Buffie The Body, Karrine Steffins—this is the hip-hop story! The art of storytelling, polemics, music, dance and rhyme. The art of words!

And while I'm on this rap history tangent, let me let you know that white folks have been instrumental in the evolution of rap/hip-hop also. Here's another piece of rap trivia—the first rap song to become a number one hit was by a white group—*Blondie* featuring Debbie Harry. In 1981 their single *Rapture* became the first rap-influenced song to reach number one on the *US Billboard Charts*, thus helping to legitimize the rap genre. Again—Revolution! Evolution! The wheels of hip-hop keep on spinnin' like *Sprewell* rims on a *Denali* truck. Why wouldn't you think homo-hop would one day rear its' head?

So here we are today, trying to define "real" hip-hop and so-called "commercial" hip-hop. Underground vs. Mainstream. KRS-One dissin' Nelly's brand of rap. What bullshyt! Let me give it to you straight no chaser! Yes! I love Ja Rule! (Homophobia and all!) But I also love that gangsta shyt that 50 Cent raps. I can't be swayed to hate one rapper just because another rapper has a beef with him! I love all of the genres of rap. I love the lyrical dexterity of Jadakiss, the rapid-fire flows of Bone Thugs and Twista, the sing-song rap of Nelly and the succinctness of Eminem's metaphors. I love rap music! I love Trick Daddy's gangsta and compassion, *"Trick loves the kids"* and TI's confident swagger. I love the underground *YouTube* battles of Nycks, *"You just mad 'cause I'm stylin' on you!"* and the worldwide acclaim of Black Eyed Peas. I love the slangulistics of E-40 and the visual creativity of Missy Elliot. Damnit! I even love the bubblegum rap of Lil Mama and I ain't afraid to admit it! The girl can flow! Is she at least 18 years old? I was just thinking … ☺

I love the intellect of Common and the ignorance of Ying Yang Twins … *"fifty-leven-times!"* Who can match Outkast's innovations? I love The Game's machismo and I especially love Lil Wayne's lyrical hunger *"… Feed me rappers or feed me beats!"* WOW! That nicca is on his way to becoming Rakim-esque! Kanye West has got rap spirituality and social commentary on lock! *"… If the devil wear Prada, Adam Eve wear nadda …"* And Bow Wow is gettin' his grown man on. Of course, I got mad love for Jay-Z, Nas, Tupac, Biggie, Ludacris, Snoop Dogg, Ice Cube, Dr. Dre, Rick Ross, Fabolous and Fat Joe and some new niccas—Plies and Flo-Rida. Check for dem Florida boyz! All dem Texas rappers workin' some shyt out! And you know P Diddy is always on his musical grind. I love all the rappers! And those hip-hop sangas—Nate Dogg, T-Pain and Akon! What! I'm as ingratiated with mainstream rap as any hetero head! So don't get it twisted! I love all the misogyny, N-word using, B-word using, H-word using, F-word using and homophobia that comes with rap music, even as I deconstruct the origin and mindset of rap lyrics and help take rap music to a better place. Why do I love it? Because rap comes from an honest place called REALITY! These young people rap about what they see and hear in their environments. We can't point the finger at them and we shouldn't be kicking them like a stray dog in the street because they used the B/H/N/F words! Where were we before they became famous? Who among the learned tried to pull their coattails back then? Mainstream rappers—keep doing your thing!!!!!!!!!!!! But peep my perspective!

Yeah, I'm ridin' this homo-hop train, but don't be confused about my sexuality! I'd love to smack Trina's phat ass, taste Foxy Brown's chocolate hue, force Jacki to moan *"O"*, make Remy Ma *"lean back"* and find out *"how many licks does it take to get to the center"* of Lil Kim's sweet spot! STRAIGHT like that! Like DJ Quik used to rap, *"I love black pussy!"* I'm reppin' this homo-hop, but I'd love to kindle MC Lyte's fire, *disturb* Shawnna's *"piece,"* climb Lauryn's Hill, play with Yo-Yo's toy, sprinkle a lil' Salt-N-Pepa on my tube steak and be Eve's Adam! Please understand! Don't get me phucked up! 'Cause it ain't about the messenger! It's about the MESSAGE!

I'm in love with this homo-hop—homo-hop from all regions of the country. This book contains homo rappers from coast to coast—from Miami to Los Angeles to New York to Detroit to Ohio to the UK! Homo-hop is a thriving genre of rap music that the mainstream has not accepted out of our cultural homophobia. Hip-hop is not dead! Hip-hop just needs to introduce new and fresh voices and stop hatin' on those who would bring their vision of hip-hop to the table. This is the goal and vision of this book. Homo-hop deserves to be heard! If you were to ask any of these homo rappers who their musical influences were/are, they would all cite the obvious legends of rap (Tupac, Biggie, Jay-Z, LL Cool J, Rakim, Salt-N-Pepa, Dr. Dre., Snoop Dogg, etc.). They have much love, respect and admiration for mainstream rappers. They just happen to be homosexual. You don't have to be homosexual to like homo-hop any more than you have to be a gang banger to like gangsta rap! Expand your mind and become eclectic in your musical tastes.

I'm a Dirty South brotha, raised in Miami, but Miami does not define my taste in rap music, because I understand that we are all one people—Black, White, Hispanic, Jewish, Asian, etc. Lucy/Eve is our eponymous mother. You feel me? Every black person in New York is only a generation or two removed from the South! The South is the backbone of the African-American experience! The South is the cradle of black folks' existence! The South is the womb of Northern progressiveness! The South is the birthplace of Call and Response, Ragtime, Jazz, Gospel, R&B ... and by extension—RAP/HIP-HOP! The South has a rich heritage of Historically Black Colleges and Universities (HBCU's), as seen in movies such as **Stomp The Yard**—a movie depicting the wonderful rhythmic intricacies of black college fraternity and sorority "stepping," which is an extension of the African drum and dance tradition with hip-hop and krump dance—and **Drumline**—a movie which displays the awesome power of black marching bands like the world has never seen! "Band geek?" Puhleazzzee! Not in the South! Get that country bumkin mentality out of your mind! You have not seen a marching band until you've seen the *Florida A&M Marching 100*! (F.A.M.U.)—Eight Drum Majors—360 members—Death March cadence into a 100 step per minute march called "the Rattler!" Super Bowl XLI halftime appearance with Prince! *(Shout out to my son Yahudah Clark (sax) and my first cousin Terry Goolsby R.I.P. (sax), both former members of FAMU's marching band. Oh, and by the way, I was a member of Bethune Cookman College's Marching Wildcats ... saxophone 1978.)*

The South birthed the Civil Rights Movement, Dr. Martin Luther King Jr., Stokely Carmichael (*Kwame Toure of Black Power/S.N.C.C./Black Panther Party*), Elijah Muhammad (*founder of the Nation of Islam and spiritual teacher of Northern*

Malcolm X and Louis Farrakhan, Five Percent Nation), Muhammad Ali and many, many other notables! As Fat Joe raps, *"Why is everybody mad at the South ...?"* Don't get it twisted! The SOUTH Bronx may be the literal birthplace of hip-hop, but its roots lie in the Dirty-Dirty (the South). And by the way, can somebody please explain to Pimp C of UGKz where the South is? You know ... the Civil War, the *Emancipation Proclamation* and which states were under Southern Confederate rule under president Jefferson Davis, the Mason-Dixon Line, time zones and all of that other ignant crap he was pontificating about that he should have learned in junior high school history and civics class! Hey Pimp C! Just for your information, if you check the history books, the "TRUE SOUTH" is Georgia, South Carolina, North Carolina, Alabama, Mississippi, Louisiana, Arkansas and Tennessee!!! Virginia, Kentucky, Florida and TEXAS are considered "secondary" southern states! Texas is part of the "pseudo-South"! Boy! You really put your foot in your mouth on that one! I don't think you'd fair too well on that TV show, *So You Think You're Smarter Than A Fifth Grader.* Check your history pimpin' ... C! If ATL is not the South, then Texas is not a part of America! Duh! Okay! Enuff ramblin'. Let's get it!

"Gayngsta" rapper/homo-thug Deadlee and author/Spiritual Advisor Khalil Amani first met in San Diego, March 29, 2007, at the HomoRevolutionTour '07. Homo to Hetero ... ESE to S.A. Nothin' but love baby!

I Said It! I Meant It! I'm Here To Represent It! Homo-Hop!

○ ○

"[Homosexual people] might be the most oppressed in the society. The term 'faggot' and 'punk' should be deleted from our vocabulary ... homosexuals are not the enemies of the people!"

—The Honorable Huey P. Newton, co-founder of the Black Panther Party.

Right off the top, let me kill the false assumption that this book was written by a fag, a queer, a punk, a homo, an AC/DC man, Down Low brotha—a homosexual—a gay man who's trying to justify his lust for the same sex! You got me twisted! I am a heterosexual black man who knows the truth about the world's fixation with homophobia—a heterosexual black man who's peeped game on all of the religious and secular arguments condemning homosexuality and found them to be bogus—a heterosexual black man who doesn't give a damn about what you think about my sexuality—a heterosexual black man who's had more pussy (by accident) than most men get (on purpose)—a heterosexual married black man with five children and a couple of possibles ... a goddamned Spades hand! That is my sexual resume/curriculum vitae! But again, it ain't about the messenger! It's about the message!

For those of you gay and lesbian folk who think I can't articulate your struggle, peep game. Every group-struggle has had people from without to help them achieve their goals. If it weren't for white people like William Lloyd Garrison, the Grimke sisters, John Brown, northern white abolitionists and many good white people along the Underground Railroad, slavery would have persisted longer than it had. If it weren't for whites and Jews like Goodman and Schwerner and their black comrade, Chaney, and the N.A.A.C.P., which was founded by Jews, segregation/Jim Crowism might have taken longer to destroy. If it weren't for coun-

8

tries coming together, Hitler might have conquered the world! It's always been about coalitions … *"Coalitions of the willing"* as George Bush put it. A male doctor/gynecologist can never have a baby, but he can deliver a baby and articulate what an expectant mother will go through in childbirth. So don't hate on this brotha because he is not homosexual, 'cause it ain't even about him! Yes! There are gay intellectuals/leaders/personalities like Keith Boykins, Davey D, Jasmyne Cannick, Da Doo-Dirty Show and the brothers of *Deep Dickollective* who have all the education, intellect, insight, consciousness, experience, rap skills and charisma to awaken the sleeping giant of homo-hop! But this is what the HIGHER POWER (God) gave me! I am not gay! (And if I was, I'd be the biggest OUT gay male you've ever seen!) I've never been to a Gay Pride Parade (although I plan on doing just that!). I don't speak for all gay/lesbian people. I am not a part of the gay and lesbian community, yet I've been blessed to speak on behalf of those gay, lesbian, bisexual and transgendered brothers and sisters who feel my message, and for that, I'm thankful! I've been blessed with spiritual knowledge about the true origins of homophobia with the intellectual/spiritual acumen to make even the simplest among us understand.

Like Bishop Don "Magic" Juan, I am a Spiritual Advisor to hip-hop. But unlike him, I have something relevant to say! I'm not trying to use Jesus as a ruse to pimp women on the D/L. Like Bishop Don "Magic" Juan, who wrote his autobiography, *From Pimpstick to Pulpit,* I too have written a memoir, *My id … Ignant & Dissfunkshunal! Life in the Yahweh Cult and the Witness Protection Program.* He was a pimp and I was pimped! We've both led controversial, dysfunctional and tumultuous lives. We both speak from life experiences coupled with knowledge and enlightenment about things beyond the 'hood. I'm six books deep to his one. He's 57 years old and I'm 47 years old. There, the similarities end. My message has great substance and if you read my work you will cosign me. For I am the spiritual voice of homo-hop—the voice of reason and rage! I bring clarity and sanity and speak truth to ignorance. I'm here for all of my "LGBT" brothers and sisters! Let me help you kill generations of homophobia.

To those black heterosexual pseudo intellectuals who argue that the Gay and Lesbian Movement is "Pimping the Civil Rights Movement"—trying to equate the Gay/Lesbian struggle with black folks' struggle—let me add my two cents. Black struggle is not the first struggle! Just read your Bible! The Israelites endured 400 years of slavery at the hands of the Egyptians. Race and class struggles are documented throughout history. So black folk ain't got a monopoly on struggle! Black struggle is not the litmus test whereby we judge the validity of all other struggles! Human and Civil Rights against any group of people is wrong! And any group of people who feel violated by society has the GOD GIVEN RIGHT to lift up their voices in protest and shout to the hills and mountaintops their grievances. This is Manifest Destiny!

"Six million Jews died in the holocaust!" *"So! Fifty million Africans died in the African 'Hellocaust'!"* It is a self-serving and ignorant debate/argument/polemic! Such bullshyt! Arrogant-assed self-serving black folk acting like their struggle is the only valid one! Got the word "struggle" in the corner like a kid who doesn't want any of his friends to play with his toys! He doesn't want to play with it until someone else wants to play with it! *"Mommy, mommy, Johnny's playin' with my toy!"* That's how a lot of black folk treat struggle—like it's theirs and theirs only! Every nation has had to deal with some funky "shit-uations!"

If anything, black folk should be on the front line of the pro-homosexual movement! As one oppressed group to others, black folk and women should be most empathetic towards gays and lesbians, having been oppressed themselves. We should not have the mentality that *"my struggle is greater than yours,"* *"you choose to be gay or lesbian, I was born black!"* and all of the other asinine debates about whose struggle merits more attention. All struggle deserves maximum attention!

The Abolitionist Movement, the Women's Suffrage Movement, the Civil Rights Movement, the Black Power Movement, the Feminist Movement, the Gay Rights Movement, Feminist Theology (Radford-Reuther), Black Liberation Theology (J. Cone), Latin American Theology (G. Gutierrez)—it's called evolution and revolution people! Humankind is EVOLVING and addressing the ills of society. Whether they be secular or religious, the learned amongst us are rethinking the ideologies of the past. It ain't about what group is "copying" another group's platform to further their own agenda. It's about a free and democratic First World society that is constantly reevaluating its policies towards all of its citizenry and challenging those policies that are clearly in violation of human and civil rights. In times past, there was a belief that black people were not fully human—perhaps $3/5^{th}$ human. We, as a society killed that myth! There is a long-standing belief that homosexuality is an abomination against God—we're working on killing that myth.

All of us were born butt-ass naked, knowing nothing. In psychological terms, our mind was a *Tabula Rasa*—a Blank Slate. And then … and then our minds were filled with all kinds of garbage. At what age did we realize that homosexuality was wrong? Think about it for a moment. What influences led you to believe that gay and lesbian love is wrong. Who taught you that? It is safe to say that our homophobia is religiously rooted.

Straight folk! Remember the DAY you realized you were HETEROSEX-UAL—the day you said to yourself, *"Am I attracted to the opposite sex?"* Remember the day you "chose" your heterosexuality? You don't? Well I don't either! As a straight man, I don't remember that "definitive," "earth-shattering," "revelatory" day in junior high school where I realized I liked girls. It just sort of was. I didn't have to make a conscious decision to be attracted to the opposite sex. I just was! There was no epiphany or revelation one day that allowed me to be attracted to girls! I just was! So why do many heterosexuals try to make the argument that homosexuality is a "chosen" lifestyle? Why can't we give the gay person the benefit of the doubt that they were actually BORN attracted to the same sex, just as a straight person was BORN attracted to the opposite sex? Why can't we accept that homosexuality is a part of the human condition—that there is absolutely nothing wrong with same-sex attraction—that homosexuality is not an aberration to human sexuality—a deviation from the norm?

It is a BELIEF that gays and lesbians CHOOSE to be homosexual. It-is-what-it-is! A BELIEF! "BELIEF" is not a concrete, proven, undeniable, uncontested, knowable, tangible fact! BELIEF is theory, hypothesis, opinion, and extrapolation—understanding about that which we have found no concrete, tangible evidence for its existence in the physical realm like "god." BELIEF is not COGNITION—KNOWING! You don't know for a fact that homosexuals "choose" their sexual preference and more and more, the scientific evidence is confirming that homosexuality is not a choice, but rather an innate biological sexual response and attraction to the same sex. Sexuality is not black and white! There are gray/gay areas. There are many "deviations/anomalies/aberrations" (if you will) in human sexuality. Homosexuality is not a deviation! How do you explain a person born with a penis and a vagina—a hermaphrodite/intersexed? How do you explain a man who's always felt like a woman and vice versa? How do you explain the little boy who loves dolls and women's clothes more than toy trucks and wearing his daddy's shoes? How do you explain the little girl who would rather wear jeans than a dress and roughhouse it with the boys instead of dressing up like mama in high-heels and make-up? You've seen children that you knew were going to be gay or lesbian and it had nothing to do with nothing! THEY WERE BORN THAT WAY! But in our simplistic understanding of human sexuality, in an attempt to rationalize homosexuality, we say these people are born with a deformity (hermaphroditic) or crazy for having aberrant thoughts about who they are. Yeah, that's it! That fits neatly into our heterosexual lunch box! Sadly, there are some homosexuals who believe that homosexuality is deviant sexual behavior—the ultimate cultural/religious brainwashing!

There are no preconceived motives in writing this book other than the bottom-line truth. If you're into being lied to, keep listening to some of these ignorant preachers or your favorite homophobic rapper/reggae artist or your favorite fag-bashing athlete. This ain't no "safe" read for the homophobe! I'm-a tear the lining out of the ass of his/her mind! I'm gonna spit it (the truth) and then quit it!

Think not that I am come to destroy the sanctity of heterosexual marriage! Nay! All is well in Heteroville. I'm here to put you up on secular/religious game. I'm here to put this ignorant and uninformed homophobic argument on blast! I'm here to tell you that everything you thought that the Bible, the church, your preacher, your mama, your favorite rapper, your favorite reggae star, your favorite athlete and society has taught you concerning homosexuality, as "sin" is a damnable lie! I'm here to tell you that every one of us has been brainwashed through Judeo-Christian teachings and that every silly thought in our heads concerning anti-homosexuality is the result of cultural conditioning, laden with religio-centric biases! I'm here to tell you that Judaism, Christianity and Islam are WRONG as hell regarding the condemnation of homosexuality and I'm going to back it up with reasoning for anyone who has an ear.

I'm not appealing to your intellectual/scholarly/religious/ed-ju-ma-cated reading of psychology, sociology, religion, philosophy or history! Forget about Freud, Yung, Skinner, Piaget, Hegel, Akbar, Tillich, Bultmann, Nietzsche, Madhubuti, Cress-Welsing, Fanon, Ben-Yochannon, Rev. Creflo Dollar and other clerics (who calls homosexuality a "perversion"), Cornel West and new-jack hip-hop scholar, Michael Eric Dyson! (No disrespect to these great thinkers.) I'm tryin' to holla at the "average Joe" who ain't well-read! I'm speaking to your base intellect and I'm doing it in a way that most of us can readily understand. My wording, my writing style—get over it! Ghetto grammar all day baby! I'm not here to impress you journalism majors with a lot of literary masturbation and pontification. Go write your own boring-ass heterocentric book and impress us with your copycat literary acumen. That ain't my lane. I'm traveling down a lonely road called *Absolute Truth*. Come on and take a ride with me, won't cha? It-is-what-it-is! Real talk!

There are literally thousands of books that have been written on homosexuality, which argue that homosexuality is a normal part of human sexuality. There are also thousands of books written to condemn homosexuality as a deviation from human sexuality. Psychiatrists, psychologists, sex therapists, politicians, and preachers have lent their voice and pen to this debate. Masters & Johnson, Anita Bryant, Dr. Ruth, Dr. Laura Schlessinger, Kinsey's *Seven Point Scale of Sexual Orientation* ... they've all weighed in on this subject *ad nauseam!* There are also books written by Afrocentric (black) scholars, which dissect the black man's fem-inization, emasculation and homosexuality as the result and byproduct of slavery, white supremacy and the severed black family. There's even a school of thought among black afrocentrists who believe that homosexuality is a "white man's dis-ease!"—that homosexuality was/is nonexistent on the continent of Africa. These black quacks deal in revisionist history, black superiority, pseudo science and reverse racism.

There are books about the size of a homosexual's brain compared with a het-erosexual's brain. They've got books of a Freudian nature that want us to believe that gay people suffered from some form of the *Oedipal/Electra Complex* in their childhood.

They've got religious books that tell us that homosexuality is condemned by a "god" that they are intimately familiar with—a "god" who loves straight people and hates gay people. But they teach, *"God loves the sinner, but hates the sin"* as though they themselves, are not sinners and homosexuality is the greatest sin imaginable. Gay "gayngsta" rapper Deadlee raps, *"Calling me a sinner. Yeah, you love me, but hate my sin. I don't need your compassion! Hate this sinner 'cause I love this sin!"* I get his point! But homosexuality is not a "sin" against God! This is the focus of this book, whether you are hetero or homo!

Sin? The Bible defines sin as "transgression [breaking] of the law" (I John 3:4). There are 613 laws and commandments in the Old Testament and some of them have been manufactured/concocted for socio-religio-political reasons! Examples? The secondary citizenry of women—social! (The creation account in Genesis 2, sin entering the world by a woman Genesis 3, the Ten Commandments Exodus 20) The calling of Israel "chosen"—political! (The whole Old Testament!) The condemning of homosexuality—religious! (Deuteronomy 23:17) Not all of these laws are from above (God).

We've been so brainwashed with negative connotations of homosexuality that we can't fathom the thought that a "god" could've made some of us instinctively/biologically attracted to the same sex! And if we do accept this premise, then we have to put homosexuality in the same category with pedophilia (child fucking), mental retardation, and physical deformity … a few of your god's little anoma-lies/aberrations/mistakes. Why can't we just accept what the **American Psychiat-ric Association (APA)** has written, according to their **Diagnostic and Statistical Manual of Mental Disorders (DSM-II/III-R/IV)**?:

The Board of Trustees of the American Psychiatric Association (APA) removed homosexuality from the Diagnostic and Statistical Manual of

Mental Disorders (DSM) in 1973 after reviewing evidence that it was not a mental disorder.... Therefore, APA opposes any psychiatric treatment, such as "reparative" or "conversion" therapy, that is based on the assumption that homosexuality per se is a mental disorder or is based on the a priori assumption that the patient should change his or her homosexual orientation.... Whereas homosexuality per se implies no impairment in judgment, stability, reliability, or general social or vocational capabilities, therefore, be it resolved that the American Psychiatric Association deplores all public and private discrimination against homosexuals in such areas as employment, housing, public accommodation, and licensing, and declares that no burden of proof shall be placed upon homosexuals ... [APA] supports and urges the enactment of civil rights legislation at the local, state, and federal level that would offer homosexual citizens the same protections now guaranteed to others on the basis of race, creed, color, etc.... supports and urges repeal of all discriminatory legislation singling out homosexual acts by consenting adults in private.

—American Psychiatric Association, *"Position Statement on Homosexuality and Civil Rights."*

See? The American Psychiatric Association (APA) is a national medical specialty society with over 40,000 members—all physicians/doctors who specialize in diagnosing and treating mental disorders and substance disorders. FORTY THOUSAND DOCTORS! Can you dig that? And then an ig-nant asshole ex-professional basketball player can come before us and say that homosexuals *"shouldn't be in the world or the United States."* This Negro has no business giving us his very uniformed and ignorant "opinion" on the gay question! *"Opinions are like assholes—everybody has one!"* Shut the fuck up and play pickup basketball nitwit!

For the laity (common folk), most of the arguments about homosexuality are too analytical and boring to read—a bunch of medical hyperbole and superfluous scientific theories. Now comes a book for the everyday person trying to navigate this subject. In no way is this work comprehensive or scholarly, but is meant to serve as a primer for some serious rethinking, re-teaching, reeducating and intelligent conversation on the subject. It is my intent to expose the origin of anti-homosexual biases—to let the homophobic reader "overstand" his or her social conditioning and religious brainwashing—to give the homosexual reader ammunition (historical and religious information) to combat the homophobia in the world and "overstand" that there is absolutely nothing wrong with any same-sex feelings that he or she is having.

The so-called "educated" have their books, pro and con. Now it is time for the not-so-formally-educated to come in contact with some information that they can sink their teeth into—a book that they can explore their fears and prejudices about homosexual love and begin to understand the origin of those biases and attitudes. My captive audience? *Hip-Hop* Heads. This book is not an indictment against every *hip-hop* head, rapper, thug, athlete, reggae rasta or religionist. It is a general indictment against the present state of *hip-hop's* commercialized acceptance of homosexual bashing in the music and culture. *Hip-hop* heads, thugs, athletes, reggae rastas and rappers aren't responsible for homophobia. They are the microcosm of a macrocosmic global pogrom that's been waged against homosexuals that has gone on far too long. Many *hip-hoppers* are just the ignorant byproduct of a world society that has perpetuated homophobia, parroting what they know not. And just as important is the misogyny (women hating) in *hip-hop*, which needs to be more thoroughly addressed and dealt with as well!

Why am I addressing this small part of American culture? First and foremost, I'm a 47year old black man who loves *hip-hop*! Secondly, I'm a cultural critic who views homophobia as one of the ills of our society like racism, sexism, and classism. Thirdly, I'm a religious scholar/spiritual advisor who's not afraid to espouse the truth against all that organized religion has taught. And fourthly, I believe *hip-hop* has the power and influence to reshape the world's understanding of homosexuality!

The vast majority of rappers are as ignorant (without knowledge) as the society in which they come from. From "Conscious" Common who rapped, *"In a circle of faggots, your name is mentioned!"* to "Gangsta" 50 Cent who rapped, *"Fuckin' faggot."* The list of rappers who have used homophobic lyrics includes, but not limited to, Jay-Z, DMX, Eminem, and Busta Rhymes.

I used to have mad respect for Bussa Bus, but ever since he got with 50 Cent to diss Ja Rule he's carried himself like he's a gangster. They asked him what he thought about gays in hip-hop and he responded by getting up and rudely excusing himself from the interview like the question offended and disgusted him! But what should we expect from an Island nigga? They are the most homophobic! Oh he's one arrogant bastard these days! Hey Busta, stop frontin' like you're a thug and cooperate with the police to help solve your friend Izzy's murder! Give his mom rest! You know who pulled the trigga nigga! Fuck your career, your 'hood status and the street code of no snitching! Give his soul rest!

"Conscious" Common and Kanye West are among the few rappers who have made statements regarding their homophobia and have taken steps to correct it. On Common's CD, *Electric Circus* Common bravely explores the reality of a gay loved one on his song *"Between Me, You & Liberation"* when he raps, *"So far we'd come, for him to tell me/as he did, insecurity held me/'Til his spirit yelled help me. How could I judge him? Had to accept him if I truly loved him/No longer, he said, had he hated himself/Through sexuality he liberated himself."* WOW! That's deep!

I am reminded of the time I met Common in Denver (2001) backstage after his and Erykah Badu's concert. I presented him with a few of my books. One of my books, *Ghetto Religiosity II: Uncovering the Naked Truth* has the same chapter that is in this book, *"Homosexuality: The Great Sin of Sodom? Deconstructing the Biblical Myth Against Homosexuality."* I have to assume that he's read it and gained some spiritual insights. There is definitely an evolution in Common's awareness from *Like Water For Chocolate* to *Electric Circus*, recorded two years apart—2000 to 2002. I'd like to think that my book helped shape his thinking on his song, *"Between Me, You & Liberation."* Coincidentally, the other book I gave Common was titled, *Ghetto Religiosity 2000: Third Millennium LIBERATION.* Hmmm? Holla at me Common!

Common and Kanye West have disposed with the use of the word faggot in their lyrics, because they have sense enough to understand that they are dissin' people who they claim they love. And yes, "faggot," like "nigga" has different meanings, depending on the context in which the word is being used. "Faggot," in rap terms, is the equivalent of a white person calling a black person a nigger—It is the ultimate put-down, the *coup de grace* (death blow) of disrespect—the emasculation of the manhood—the feminizations of the 'hood man's psyche. Go to these Internet rap blogs and you will see such phrases as "no homo," and "that's gay." These Internet bloggers are so ig-nant that many of their "opinions" come down to simple name-calling when discussing *hip-hop.* Any rapper that they feel is not "keepin' it real" or "reppin' their set to the fullest" is gay. And by gay they don't mean in the homosexual sense, but rather gay as weak (as they believe homosexuals are). *Hip-hop* needs a serious chin-checking (punch) when it comes to homophobia and misogyny and I'm here to throw an overhand right … right to the jaw of the *hip-hop* paradigm and knock it straight the fuck out! Yeah, some of y'all might be mad, *"cause I'm stylin' on you!"*

Now it is time for *hip-hop* to know the truth about homosexuality and embrace the lifestyle/culture—not that heteros and homos gotta sit around and hold hands and sing *Kum-By-Yah*, but rather to allow their voices to be heard in mainstream media (MTV, BET, VH-1, The Source, Vibe, XXL Mag, Spin, Rolling Stone, etc.). An openly gay/lesbian person needs to accept an award at the Grammys, the VMA's, the BET awards, the Source awards, the American Music Awards, etc.

Gay bashing is so cliché, so unoriginal, so inauthentic, so juvenile, so ignorant, so religiously misunderstood, so culturally demented and so very Twentieth Century! Homophobia stands as the last bastion of ignorance in human growth and development. Many of us who call gays "fags" only do it to validate our masculinity and to make sure that no one mistakes us for being gay. And then we walk and talk that *"I don't give a damn what people think or say about me!"* Yeah, right! I wanna see Snoop Dogg do a record with gay rapper Deadlee, whose sound is reminiscent of an Ice-T. I wanna see Missy Elliot do a record with lesbian rapper FELONi, who has the lyrical dexterity of an MC Lyte, a Foxy Brown or a Remy Ma! Don't worry about what the world thinks about your sexuality. Do you!

Most of us don't even know why we hate gays and lesbians! A gay or lesbian person never called you a nigger, a cracker or a spic—never burned a cross on your lawn—never hung you from a tree—never enslaved you—never called you a "fucking heterosexual!"—Never heterosexual-bashed you or beat you up in the schoolyard for being straight! Let's face it! Many of us hate gay people because we've been conditioned to hate them! By our actions, we copy, parrot, ape, and regurgitate the cultural/religious bullshyt handed down to us! We are about as freethinking as the parrot who says, *"Polly wanna cracker."* Dumb-ass bird doesn't know the English language! He is IMITATING sounds! When we diss gays and lesbians, we are IMITATING cultural "sounds"/garbage! The parrot doesn't know why he says, *"Polly wanna cracker!"* The homophobe doesn't know why he says, *"Fuck all fags!"* The NBA basketball player doesn't know why he hates gays! He's got millions of dollars, fame, and adulation from adoring fans, a beautiful family and lifestyle, but doesn't have enough sense to know that his homophobic ranting won't fly in a culturally diverse society, especially in a city like Miami, which has a large gay community. What was this Negro thinking? He wasn't thinking—logically! Now you wanna apologize? No! Go sit your ass in the corner and put on your dunce cap, you ignorant homophobic nincompoop!

When questioned at length, the homophobe might try the religious route (as not to appear ignorant) and feign religiously astute and try to tell you what the Bible has to say about homosexuality, but upon closer inspection, he's merely regurgitating the pseudo-religiosity of his ignorant religious upbringing. Ask him to take you through the Bible and cogently construct the argument against homosexuality and you'll see that he is indeed ignorant about biblical scriptures.

His greatest retort might be the nursery rhyme inspired cliché, *"God created Adam and Eve, not Adam and Steve!"* Oh, you profound muthafucka you! Not!

One hundred years from now, the homosexual question will have been asked and answered! The verdict? They will look back at us 21st Century idiots and ask the question, *"You mean they really were against gays and lesbians marrying? They really thought that gays and lesbians 'chose' to be homosexual? How stupid!"* They will view homophobia with the same disdain that we view slavery and prohibition. We can hardly believe that one people enslaved another people or that there was a time when alcohol was illegal. Homosexuality, along with marijuana will be legal and an accepted part of their society by the year 2107.

"The truth ain't for everybody," they say. But I say the truth is for everybody. Deal with it or get ran the hell over by it! That's what's about to happen as you peruse this book!—Raw, unadulterated, in-your-face truth. If your eyes are too virginal and holy to deal with a curse word here and there, put this book down now! Some say my writing is profane. I agree! But let me add Muhammad Ali's very eloquent analysis of his own being: *"Profane, yet profound!"* Sometimes a curse word is not just a curse word. Sometimes you've got to shout your message from the rooftop to be heard. I'm fuckin' shouting! Holla if you hear me!

A Man Ain't Nothin' But A Homo!

○ ○

"I still hear people say that I should not be talking about the rights of lesbian and gay people and I should stick to the issues of racial justice … But I hasten to remind them that Martin Luther King Jr. said, 'Injustice anywhere is a threat to justice everywhere.' I appeal to everyone who believes in Martin Luther King Jr.'s dream to make room at the table of brother—and sisterhood for lesbian and gay people."

—*The Honorable Coretta Scott King, wife of Martin Luther King Jr.*

That's right! I said it! A man ain't nothin' but a Homo! What am I talking about? Listen up. Some heterosexual men love to gay-bash. They call homosexuals *fags, booty-bandits, rump-rangers,* and *brown-towners.* Their sexual activity is called *goin' down the dirt road, goin' to shitty city, living in Brownsville,* and *traveling the Hershey highway.* Oh how some of us love to fag-bash. But let me tell you something, all of you heterosexual males. You are more Homo than a homosexual ever could be! What? That's right! From the time you came out of your mama's womb you were a Homo. The minute they put those blue booties and that blue blanket and that blue bonnet on your head, you were being conditioned to be Homo. What? Yeah! "Homo-centric" and "Homo-psychic,"—not necessarily homosexual.

Homo comes from Latin meaning *"man"* and *"same."* Homo means *"of the same sex."* Homocentric means having the same center. (i.e.. likes, dislikes, surroundings, hobbies, etc.) Homo-psychic is a word I created to describe the same mind-set—the way males think in general terms. All of us are considered *Homo sapiens* and we come from an earlier man, *Homo erectus.* Homo is a part of our make-up. Ninety-nine percent of boys and men experience homoeroticism, which is the sexual attraction for one's own sex, as in homosexuality or through masturbation. Statistically, between 18%-42% of men have had some type of homosexual experience. As Jamie Foxx so bravely put it (paraphrase), *"I got issues when I look at Prince!"* The man is beautiful!

But I ain't talkin' about homosexuality in the literal sense. I'm talking about a Homo-centric and a Homo-psychic mind that men are bound by, which will not allow them act, live, think, feel, and do that which is contrary to the male-mind, which is tantamount to being homosexual or "soft." Most heterosexual men are guilty of the *Homo-centric Idea*. They are conditioned to be male-centered and they are programmed to do the male-thing. This is what makes them Homos. Juxtapose the heterosexual male with the homosexual male and it becomes clear that, at least in action, the homosexual is more "Hetero" and the heterosexual is more "Homo." The homosexual male, by his very nature, acts as Hetero-centric. "Hetero" only means "other" and "different." No one will deny that homosexual men, in general, "act" "different" than heterosexual men (with the exception of the new homo-thug.) Many homosexual men have "feminine" mannerisms. Homosexual men, for the most part, are not conditioned by the Homocentric or same idea of manhood that heterosexual men are conditioned by. It is probably better stated that homosexual men "reject" the homocentric idea of manhood that heterosexual men are conditioned by. Many homosexual males will engage in so-called "feminine" professions. These would include being a nurse, beautician, make-up artist, fashion designer, a love for the arts, ballet dancing, sewing, cooking, cleaning, dressing well, grooming well, cheer leading, and childcare nurturer. Homosexual males may show open signs of affection through hugging, kissing and crying. These are generalities of the homosexual male. This is not to say that the heterosexual male will not engage in these activities. Neither does it suggest that all homosexual men display signs of affection. Some homosexual men are very masculine (think homo-thug). It merely suggests that the heterosexual male, by his environment, is conditioned not to be feminine, which in turn, makes him Homo-centric or of the same center—the male center. How many of our mothers told us as little boys, *"Boys don't cry!"?* How many of our fathers told us, *"Be a man! Hit him back! You can take it! It'll make you a man. Stop being a sissy!"?* Our psychologically ignorant parents conditioned us to withhold emotion. How many of us as boys played with baby dolls and "girl things" and our parents took them from us because they feared that we would become homosexual? I can personally testify to this ignorant parental phenomenon.

As a teenager, I was considered somewhat feminine. Actually, I was more androgynous. It was nothing for me to play hopscotch with the girls and tackle football with the guys. I could watch the soap operas and discuss them with any girl and then go out and play baseball with the boys. I used to wear tights and take ballet lessons with my baby sister and then go roughhouse it with the fellas. And I loved the hell out of doing housework, especially washing the dishes. It made my nails so clean and shiny with a clear coat of polish. I guess I was some kind of kid! I used to go to the movies during my summer teen years and sit in the theater with napkins in my hands from crying over movies like *Butterflies Are Free* and *Bless The Beast And The Children*. I would cry with the same fury that any woman would cry. Of course I did this alone because I thoroughly understood that my male teenage buddies would shun me if they saw me crying over a movie. By 14, the sex rules and the acceptable social norms for men had been ingrained in my psyche. I knew the heterosexual mind. I presumed that my parents (at least my father) thought I was on the verge of being homosexual for my ballet dancing and house cleaning activities. Was I wrestling with my sexuality at sixteen? Was there any confusion in my mind as to whom I was attracted to? Hell no! I knew I was not homosexual. I knew I liked girls but I also knew I liked doing some of those "girlie" things. Looking back, I think I was blessed to have access to halfway good information about sex. At 15, I'd read this book my mom had tucked away in a drawer by some folks named *Masters & Johnson*. I learned all about fellatio, cunnilingus, foreplay, masturbation, and sex. I read all of my mother's *True Romance* magazines and had masturbated to my first soft-porn picture … a picture of a man and a woman making love in an empty apartment in a book called, *The Last Tango In Paris*. I knew that I was 100% heterosexual.

My father made my mother take me out of ballet because according to him, *"That boy's gonna be a faggot! I don't want that in my family!"* That same year I showed him my sexuality. This particular day my girlfriend and I skipped school during lunch and went to my house for a steamy sex-a-thon. My girlfriend had just gotten off her period and we were hot as fire to get it on. Soon as we hit the front door we started ripping each other's clothes off. Mom and pops were at work … I thought. We moved the cocktail table back while panties and bra and blouse and shirts were flung and draped over lampshades. We were fuckin'! All of a sudden I hear a car door slam but I'm too involved to peep over the couch and look out the window. It's probably the neighbors. A few seconds later, I hear my parent's voices coming up the sidewalk. Fear strikes my ass as I jump up and try to gather the evidence of our fuck-fest. Too late! When they open the door the smell of sex is in the air and our clothes are still strewn everywhere. My girlfriend is hiding in my bedroom closet and I'm in the bathroom trying to figure my way out of this situation. All I have on is my jeans ... dick limper than-a-mug! My father is going to kill me! A minute or two goes by and I hear my mother telling my father that I'm here ... with "that girl." He called me out of the bathroom and gave me the scare of my life. He threatened that he would deal with me later on when he came home from work. My mom was too sick to say much. But you know what? He never said another word about it until this very day! I guess he was relieved to find out that his son wasn't a faggot. I digressed to make a point about our roles as males.

Again, a heterosexual male ain't nothin' but a Homo. How many men do you know that aren't afraid to be human and cry when crying is warranted? The only time men cry is when their mother dies! How many times has a woman been on a date at the movies with a man and seen a sad movie and he didn't cry? Where are the man's emotion, compassion, sympathy and empathy for the characters? Does he not understand the tragedy before him? Shit! I cried on *Crooklyn, Schindler's List, Soul Food, Purple Rain, How Stella Got Her Groove Back* and I boohooed like a baby on *The Color Purple!* I cry in front of my woman. It doesn't make me less of a man. It makes me more of a human being and more of the Hetero-centric mind that many homosexual men have. And what's worse is that many women help perpetuate the stereotype of male/masculinity as stoic creatures who must remain "hard." Some women shun the "soft" brotha. The sista rapper, MC Lyte used to rap, *"Gotta get a ruff-neck!"* The brotha has to be hard-core to the bone. He must suppress all emotion.

Heterosexual men are Homo-psychic and Homocentric by condition. In sports, males show Homo-psychic and Homocentric affection by slapping one another on the rear-end, high-fives, hugging, and game winning pile-ons. In the context of team sports, males can touch one another on the butt and not appear to be homosexual. But these same men will fag-bash a homosexual in dance tights for his femininity. He doesn't relate to the fact that if he's a football or baseball player, he too, wears tights. Even in basketball, up until the late '80s, teams wore some tight fitting shit that looked like those hot-pants we wore in the '70s ... looked like the male version of the Daisy Dukes shorts! Not only were they tight, they rode way up on the legs! Thank God for the baggies they wear now. Football pants and baseball pants are as formfitting as any tights a ballet dancer might wear. But the difference is the stereotype involved with wearing ballet tights as opposed to football or baseball tights. The male ballet dancer is homosexual. The football player is heterosexual. But when we look at the mind-set of these individuals, the roles are reversed. The heterosexual male becomes Homocentric in his thinking and the Homosexual male becomes Hetero-centric in his actions. So who's really the Homo here? The heterosexual male is bound by his conditioning of the male paradigm so, in essence, he becomes Homocentric or centered on the same male thinking processes. On the other hand, the homosexual male, not being bound by the male paradigm, freely allows himself (at the risk of being ridiculed) to explore the Hetero-centric psyche, which is the different or feminine side of his nature. Only in sexual orientation is he Homo. For the heterosexual male, he is only Hetero by sexual orientation. His mind is Homo.

Another example of the homocentric mind in the heterosexual male is evident in music. Rap is especially given to the homocentric mind-set of the heterosexual male. There are graphic illusions to homosexuality from so-called hard-core Hetero-rappers. When Dr. Dre. raps in reference to Luke of Two-Live Crew, *"Gap teeth in your mouth so my dick's got ta fit!"* What does Dr. Dre. mean by such a homosexual lyric? He would tell you and I that Luke giving him a blow-job is a way of showing disrespect for Luke and his rapping—diss his masculinity, his manhood, effeminizing him. He could have said, "I'll kick your ass in a street fight." But instead Dr. Dre chose to play out his fantasy of having Luke suck his dick. What does this say about a man who would let another man perform fellatio on him? Is this not some perverted form of homoeroticism? I think so. A follow-up question would be; If Luke did perform oral sex on Dr. Dre., does Dr. Dre. become aroused by Luke's fellatio? And, if so, does that make Dr. Dre. homosexual as well as Homo-psychic? I think so. In that same song, Dr. Dre. and Snoop Doggy Dogg rap, *"Luke's bendin' over so Luke's gettin' fucked! ... one-eight-seven with my dick in your mouth! ... with my nuts on yo' tonsils while you're rappin' at yo' whack-ass concert! ... Eazy E can eat a big phat dick, Luke can eat a phat dick!"* In their minds they are doing the ultimate diss by trying to emasculate Luke and Eazy E of their manhood and turn them into effeminate rappers who suck the dicks of the hard-core gangsta rappers, but a "Sigmund Freud" might suggest to us that these rappers have a latent homosexual desire brought on by a severed relationship with their fathers. They may be suffering from some forms of the *Oedipus Complex,* and *Castration Anxiety.* Why else would some of these rapper want us to know that they would like to have another man perform oral sex on them or tell us the size of their penises? Snoop claims he's packin' ten inches. Hammer showed us in his *Pumps and a Bump* video that he's either packin' or stuffing his G-string. DJ Quik informs us that his *"dick's a size seven but if the bitch is fine it can stretch to a nine ..."*

The old feud between LL Cool J and Canibus is another example of homocentric thinking. Canibus raps against LL, *"Study my rhymes, then you laid your vocals after mine! That's a bitch move, something a Homo-rapper would do! ... 99% of your fans wear heels!"* There are a few things that are disturbing about Canibus' lyrics. His lyrics are paradoxical. I hear homophobia and misogyny (hatred of women) in his lyrics. Out of one side of his mouth his misogynistic ranting is subliminally suggested with the use of the word "bitch," a derogatory term used to designate the female gender. What is a "bitch move?" ... Something a female would do? Out of the other side of his mouth he insinuates that LL Cool J is a "Homo-rapper." At that time, were there any known "Homo-rappers" out there? I'd sure like to know! His lyrics suggest that he hates women and homosexuals. If this is true, what does that make Canibus? Perhaps asexual? And, what's wrong with having the validation of a female audience? Why does Canibus think that rap must be validated by males? Could it be that Homocentric and Homo-psychic mind-set? I think so. When he is performing does he enjoy looking into the eyes of male fans more than female fans? If the answer is yes, this is homocentrism. I'm pretty sure that Canibus is not homosexual or asexual (as far as I know), so why does he feel the need to dog the female segment of his listeners? What we have is a heterosexual male with a homocentric mind-set.

In fairness to rappers Canibus, Quik, Dre. and Snoop, in their ignorance, they are actually carrying on a 3000 year old male penis practice in a perverted kind of way. The ancients swore righteously by their penises. These rappers "swear" that they have the biggest, best penises, as though the prerequisite for being a rapper is to be well endowed.

A man ain't nothin' but a Homo! The homocentric idea is everywhere present. This is also true of our various religious beliefs. It doesn't matter if you're Jewish, Christian or Muslim. Your religion is homocentric. The representations and symbols of your religion are homocentric. The love you express towards your god is homocentric. Even your god is homocentric! All of your religious heroes/prophets are male-Homo-centric. From your male gods Yahweh, Jehovah, and Allah to Abraham, Isaac, Jacob, Moses, David, Solomon, Jesus, Muhammad, and Buddha, we worship from a male-Homo-view of the Deity. James Brown used to sing a song, *"This is a man's, man's man's world."* He was right. Your very salvation is in the hands of a male god! Yeah, I hear you trying to argue that God is a spirit. The spirit god is a New Testament invention! Let me be blunt and tell you that *that's* theological B/S! If God is a spirit why do you call the Deity, Father, God, He, and Him? Why do you use masculine pronouns/nouns to define "It?" Why don't you use Mother, Goddess, She or Her? Doesn't feel comfortable to you does it? The truth of the matter is that the god of the Old Testament is a Man! The ancient Israelites didn't see him as a spirit. This is clearly evident by the vivid accounts they give of their meeting with their male god. Have you read the Old Testament lately? He is clearly male-man. Read Daniel 7:9 where God (the Ancient of Days) is described as an old, bearded man. In Exodus 24:9-11, Moses and the elders meet God face-to-face and have dinner with "Him." That's just one example. There are many. Even the Adam and Eve story describes God as "walking" in the garden in the cool of the day. And just what is meant when God says, *"Let us make man in our image, after our likeness?"* A person would have to be devoid of the English language to make the God of the Old Testament a spirit. Howard Eilberg-Schwartz, in his book, *God's Phallus* (penis) writes: ... *the use of the pronoun "he" cannot be dismissed as meaningless. It indicates that people conceptualize God as masculine (25).* Spinoza, in his Theologico-Political Treatise writes: *The law of Moses ... nowhere prescribes the belief that God is without a body [as in a spirit], or even without form or figure ... the Bible clearly implies that God has a form [as in a man] ... (59).* See? I'm tryin' to tell you!

This male-god that we worship creates all and condemns those who sin. And we males, homosexual and heterosexual, desire the love of this male god. There are even illusions in the Book of Ezekiel to God having a sexual relationship with Israel (16:8). Israel and Judah are spoken of as an adulterous wife and God as the jealous husband. In the New Testament, the male Christian desires the love of another man. The son—Jesus. Our male-love for the male-son is idealistic of the homocentric idea. The father is male. The son is male. And this male god has given human-males charge over females and all other creatures. This is the order of our paternalistic-sexist-homocentric religion. Not only are men the rulers and "maintainer of women" (as the Holy Qu'ran teaches), men also share the responsibility for the salvation of women and children. Men mostly lead prayers and the family blessing comes through the man. The man is the head of the wife and sits at the head of the table. He "wears the pants" in his house and he is the "king of his castle." The male god has relegated his female creation to subjugation and second-class citizenship. The male god blames the sins of the world on his lesser creation, the woman (Genesis 3:16, I Timothy 2:9-15). The male god made the male-man first and then from the male, which he created, he made a "wo-man" or a "woe"-(troubled) man. She is a "fe-male" or a "fee"-male. She must pay a "fee" in the form of blood once a month for her sin in the garden. Only a male-god could create some shit like this! The woman, in essence, was created from recycled goods. This is the suggestion offered by being created from the side-rib of Adam. The miracle of the male god and his religion is that women, for centuries have bought into their second-rate existence with that tired-ass cliché, *"God did not create the woman from Adam's back, to be in back of him. Neither did he cre-*

ate the woman from the chest of Adam, to be in front of him. God created Eve from his side to be equal with him. "Well guess what silly-nillies? God DID NOT create Adam from anything that Eve ever had! ... Front, back, side, rib, womb ... nothing! And if Eve, or women are the equal of men, why do men rule everything? It is the homocentric mind-set! From orthodox Judaism where women cannot be priests, elders or rabbis to the Christian Catholic church where women cannot be priests, bishops, or popes to Islam where women cannot be imams. How do women convince themselves that they are equal partners in the Kingdom of God? Even the aspired place of Christians, the "King"-dom of God is homocentric. Why not the "Queendom" of God? Again, it is the homocentric idea in full effect. *"There is neither Jew nor Greek ... male nor female: for ye are all one in Christ Jesus."* This is a utopian idea from another planet!

The preacher's upright, elongated, rectangular pulpit is a symbol of the homocentric paradigm. It is a phallic symbol ... a male penis. So is the cross—another phallic symbol. The phallic symbol or male penis is to be worshipped. In Japan and other parts of the Orient, you can see phallic worship. There are shrines and temples set up with all sizes and shapes of penises in them. There are huge monuments of erect penises which the people come to a pray for fertility. This is happening today! Whether overtly or covertly, we worship the male penis. The *Washington Monument* in Washington D.C. is a phallic symbol. It is called an obelisk. But in reality it's just a big dick erected and "erect" that's indicative of the homocentric paradigm of our Homo-centric-male government ran by mostly (White) men. This is our phallic worship! In ancient Egypt the obelisk was the penis of the black god Osiris, which Isis worships and conceives the child Horus by a wooden replica of Osiris' penis after his death. The phallic-obelisk-penis has always been worshipped as the divine symbol of procreation and eternal life. So reverenced was the penis that even the ancient Jews swore by their dicks. What? Believe it! In Genesis 24:1-4 Abraham tells his servant Eliezar to, *"Put, I pray thee, thy hand under my thigh and I will make thee swear by the Lord, the God of heaven ..."* In Genesis 47:29-31 Jacob asks his son Joseph to *"... put, I pray thee, thy hand under my thigh, and deal kindly and truly with me [in other words, swear to me-verse 31] ..."* If you are stuck in the literal 2007 world you read these passages as folks touching folk's thighs and swearing. But what you must do is go back circa 1800 B.C.E. and deal with the customs of the ancient Jews. When you do this, your research will show you that it was customary for a man to hold another man's penis and swear to tell the truth. The word "thigh" is a euphemism for a man's penis, dick, cock, Johnson, or whatever you want to call it. Research the word "thigh" in *The Interpreters Dictionary of the*

Bible (R-Z) and *The Eerdmans Bible Dictionary* for starters. They'll break you off something.

A man ain't nothin' but a Homo! Our government is male-Homo-centered. The Freemasons, Shriners and college fraternities thrive on the homocentric idea. I attended *Bethune-Cookman College* back in '78. I played in the band. Prior to my attending that college the band went by the name of *The Marching "Men" of Cookman.* Women were not allowed in the marching band! The year I joined we liberated the band of that sexist practice. We became *The Marching Wildcats.* Guys-night-out and male bonding is about Homo needs. From the time we are born we are placed into categories and given a script to follow. Most males will follow the script to the letter. They will enjoy "male" things. Their psyche will remain Homo (same). Their attitudes about male-homosexuality and femininity will remain Homo. Many will castigate the homosexual for having a Hetero-psyche. The next time you see someone who you perceive as homosexual, think about the Homo in you!

To My Athletes ...

It wouldn't be right if I didn't take a minute and holla at my athletes, male and female, amateur and professional—baseball, basketball, football, soccer, hockey, boxing, mixed martial arts, track & field, volleyball, golf, tennis, lacrosse, wrestling, weight lighting, Xtreme sports, skateboarding, surfing, swimming, bodybuilding, cycling, skiing, hiking, pool, bowling, poker, chess, etc. Hip-hop/rap has influenced most sports in general and the professional sports of football and basketball specifically.

Examples of professional sports figures who have been bitten by the hip-hop/ rap bug include the whole 1985 Chicago Bears football team who recorded a rap song called the **Super Bowl Shuffle**, which was a Billboard Hot 100 single and nominated for a Grammy, Shaquille O'Neal, whose rap album **Shaq-Fu** sold over two-million copies, Chris Webber's never released album **Gangsta Gangsta**, Ron Artest's **My World**, Andre Rison's **NFL Jams**, Gary Payton's **Livin' Legal & Large**, Kobe Bryant's **Thug Poet**, Roy Jones' **Body Head Anthem,** Tracy Hudson's (T-Hud) **Tru Luv**, Famouz's **Ghetto Passport**, Tony Parker's **L'effet Papillon**, Allen Iverson's **Non-Fiction** and Dana Barros/Cedric Ceballos' **Ya Don't Stop.** Ballers, living out their fantasy as rappers!

Recently, ex-NBA player Tim Hardaway ran off his mouth about how he hated gay people and so forth and so on, only to backtrack and publicly apologize for his idiotic homophobic rant. No wonder why many gay and lesbian professional athletes won't come out of the closet! It is this mentality that keeps professional sports athletes a prisoner of their sexuality. Depending on what sport you play, homosexuality is a no-no. If you're a tennis star or a figure skater or a women's basketball player there is no major repercussions for revealing your homosexuality. But if you're a football, baseball or basketball player you'd be better served to remain in the closet! Most of these sports figures come out after they retire. There are/were many gay and lesbian professional athletes, most notably John Amaechi (NBA), David Kopay (NFL), Billy Bean (MLB), Rudy Galindo (Figure Skating), Billy Jean King (Tennis), Greg Louganis (Diving), Roy Simmons (NFL), Martina Navratilova (Tennis), Geert Blanchart (Speed Skating), Brian Orser (Figure Skating), Sue Wicks (WNBA), Sheryl Swoopes (WNBA),

Michele Van Gorp (WNBA), Tom Wadell (Olympian & founder of Gay Games) and many, many more and others who have not announced their homosexuality.

There is no escaping homosexuality! Whether you're an athlete, hip-hop head or in the military, gay and lesbian people are part of every facet of American culture. Athletes! Get over it and get a life! Stop being presumptuous and thinking that a gay man in the shower with you wants to suck your dick! Some of y'all act like gays and lesbians have no discrimination in their tastes—they'll have any and everybody who'll have them! Some of you professional athletes are uglier than Dennis Rodman, but have the nerve to be homophobic! If it weren't for your money and lifestyle you'd hardly get any pussy! Are you really worried about a gay or lesbian athlete coming on to you? Are you worried that a gay man might eye-phuck you in the shower? How many times have you eye-phucked a woman and tried to lay your rap game down, only to be rejected? Should that woman have slapped the shyt out of you for talking to her? Well, it's the same thing if a gay or lesbian person came on to you! You shouldn't be offended and repulsed by his or her actions. A simple, "thanks but no thanks" and a smile should deaden that situation. I've been hit on all my life by gay men! I'm a gay man magnet! But I've never had a confrontation with a gay man when I told him I was straight. I've never had to fight a gay man because he tried to holla at me. It's actually flattering when someone thinks you're attractive—male or female. If you're confident in your sexuality it's really nothing to trip on.

Athletes are fashioned to be role-models. How many straight professional athletes have gay or lesbian friend? How many of us could kick it with a gay person and not worry about what people will think about our sexuality? It is time for straight professional athletes to take a stand against homophobia. Do some public service announcements (PSA's) about bigotry and homophobia. Who's gonna talk shyt about Lebron James addressing homophobia? How many NBA players were outraged at Tim Hardaway's comments? There should have been public outrage the size of Imus times three! This "nappy-headed" Negro should have been made a pariah for speaking such venom!

Get your mind right professional athletes because the day is coming that an openly gay professional football, baseball or basketball player is going to come on the scene and he ain't gonna take your homophobic shyt! He ain't gonna be soft, effeminate and stereotypically flaming. He's gonna be someone who's hard, tough, aggressive and very good at his sport—perhaps a brotha you wouldn't wanna meet in a dark alley. Now let's PLAY BALL!

The Origin of Our Homophobia

It doesn't matter what ghetto you were raised in or what 'hood/barrio/project or Island you came from, or what "set" you rep or the fact that you've never stepped foot in a church all of your life—It doesn't matter if you call yourself and nigga, a wigga or a trigga pullin' nigga or a wigga with a super-fine figga—It doesn't matter if you're from the upper echelon of society—the 'burbs of 90210—It doesn't matter if you're from the progressive North, the liberal West, the Bible-belt Midwest or the Country-ass Dirty South—you have been indoctrinated against homosexuality! It doesn't matter if you were raised with a silver spoon up your ass! Our Judeo-Christian society raised us to be homophobic—overtly and covertly. We have all been influenced by the "Good Book," the Bible. Our country was founded on biblical principles that still govern our morality. It is in this book that we trust to be God's Word—the truth. We believe, without question, every story, myth, parable, psalm, and gospel. As the symbol of our spirituality/faith, the most gangsta rapper can be seen sporting a crucifix (cross). He is a Christ believer, even though he may not buy into all of the trimmings of organized religion. The very fact that rappers wear crucifixes and "Jesus pieces" around their necks lets us know that they have been exposed to Christianity/religion from a little child.

Many of our preachers, the supposed "great communicators" of God's Word laid down the foundation for our homophobia. From the pulpit, many of them have spewed venom against homosexuality, convincing us that God is against gays and lesbians by citing a few bullshyt passages from the Bible to back up their claim. Yes, I said "bullshyt passages" from the Bible! They are bullshyt when you come to understand their origins. It is from these very, very few scriptures that homophobia enters the annals of human history. Many of our preachers, in their ignorance, have accepted all that was handed down to them concerning homosexuality. Even those that went to seminary school and studied the history of religion/Judaism—having come in contact with *"Pseudepigraphal," "Apocryphal,"* and *"Gnostic"* texts—*"The Sayings Gospel Q"*—having studied the *"Dead Sea Scrolls,"* the *"Nag Hammadi"* writings—having knowledge of the *"Secret Gospel of Mark"* (a text that hints that Jesus "might" have been a homosexual, according to

30

one Professor Morton)—having studied the writings of our great African/Christian church father, St. Augustine, as he wrestled with his own homosexuality, as he wrote some of the most prolific Christian doctrine on his way to sainthood—many of our preachers come away as stupid … as ignorant … as brainwashed … as biased … as homophobic as a nicca from the 'hood! They've got all of the knowledge, all of the information at their disposal, all of the controversy surrounding the advent of Christianity, yet they are too chicken-shyt to move their congregations beyond the homophobia that preceded them into the ministry! They ain't tryin' to be controversial! They ain't tryin' to be progressive! They ain't tryin' to be freethinking! They ain't tryin' to rock the boat! They ain't tryin' to rethink the ignorance of ages gone by! They ain't tryin' to tell the goddamned truth concerning homosexuality and the bullshyt reasons why the Bible supposedly condemned homosexuality! Nay! They are stuck on a 3,000-year-old lie! They are stuck in the city of Sodom! But I'm gonna kill it dead for anyone who has an ear! You smell me?

The origin of our homophobia was birthed some 3,000 years ago by a nomadic and freebooting people—a people without a country—a people who claimed to have divinely inspired truths that were foreign to the nations—a people who came on the world stage as the bringers of light (knowledge) when, in fact, they were thieves, plagiarists and copiers of all that is called "holy." They became the masters of lying in a holy manner! (Nietzsche) The so-called "holy men" among them conspired to overthrow the religions of the people they encountered by writing laws that were aimed at suppressing the religious practices and the sexual appetites of their people. A grand conspiracy I tell you!

They were called "Hebrews"—the people who "crossed over," "crossed a boundary," and "wandered." All of their stories are reminiscent of Sumerian, Babylonian, Egyptian, Canaanite, and Persian myths that predate the Bible by one thousand years! Can you feel me? It is from these copiers, the Hebrew/Jewish nation that we have arrived at our present attitudes and biases about homosexuality—from a bunch of ignorant men from ages gone by. What the hell did they know about sex and sexuality? Nadda! You've got a problem with what I just wrote? Your problem is with your lack of history—religious history to be more specific.

The dissin' of homosexuality is a religious hoax, rooted in ancient Jewish folklore, written by their priests, who forged God's signature to give their sentiments authenticity and validity. A simply investigation into the matter makes one conclude that the Bible isn't the all-inspired Word of God, but rather an amalgamation of nameless/anonymous writers who concocted the homosexual myth in the name of their god for a specific purpose. The myth against homosexuality in the Bible has about as much truthfulness as Uncle Remus' *Briar Rabbit* and *Aesop's Fables*! It is these same liars that concocted the "Hamitic Myth!" *(A bullshyt fragmented myth in Genesis 9 that teaches that black 'Hamitic/African' people were supposed to be subservient/slaves to white people and taught by Southern white racist preachers during slavery times to keep the African in check. This myth laid the moral pretext for the enslavement of millions of African people! ... Right out of your "holey" Bible!).* It is a lie! Straight like that! But because it's in the Bible, we believe it. Bullshyt to the tenth power I tell you! The Bible, in its misreading, has been used to enslave African people and now it is being used to send gays/lesbians to hell. Everything we believe we feel about homosexuality is rooted in the Bible. I officially charge some of the Bible writers as homophobes, Negrophobes and misogynists! The homosexual myth is a lie!

Some of our parents told us, *"Don't play with yourself (masturbate) or you'll go blind!" "Don't play with yourself or you'll get hairy palms!"* Some of our preachers refer to the story of Onan in the Bible, who, when about to ejaculate (cum), pulled out of the woman and shot his wad (sperm) on the ground (Genesis 38:9-10). The technical/sexual term is called *Coitus Interruptus.* God killed him for "pulling out!" Thus, we get—"masturbation is bad." Look where TWO muthafuckin' scriptures got us! Shame, guilt, and fear for exploring the erogenous zones of one's own body! Such a simple story, written 3,000 years ago, that is still parroted in the pulpit today to keep us from sexual experimentation. It might have worked on some of us, but, for the most part, we found out that they were LIARS! We didn't go blind or get hairy palms! God did not strike us dead for pulling out and ejaculating in the air! And so it is with the homosexual myth in the Bible. Boy have we been duped into some ig-nant shyt!

It doesn't matter if you're the most hardcore gang banger out here! Somewhere in your upbringing the message was thoroughly ingrained in your psyche to view homosexuality as sin. But had it not been for the Bible's polemic (argument) against homosexuality, you wouldn't be dissin' gays and lesbians like you do. If the Bible had not first dissed homosexuality, we wouldn't be having this discussion in 2007. So understand that anti-homosexuality's mother is the Jewish nation's concocted myth. Just keep reading and you shall get to the meat of historical homophobia and come away with a clear understanding of how the world came to dislike homosexuals—just keep reading and you will understand how some ignorant men who claimed they were speaking and writing on God's behalf, who could barely read and write themselves—who couldn't articulate in any formal manner where babies came from—came to believe that same-sex attraction was an abomination (evil) unto the Lord—a book (Old Testament), which condemns man-on-man love, but says nothing about lesbianism—says nothing about incest between a man and his daughter!—condones polygamy (multiple wives)—condones intermarriage between first cousins. All these things were going on back then, as they are going on today. But the move to condemn homosexuality was not just a religious one, but a political move, which was to insure the growth and existence of the Jewish nation. Just keep reading!

Is the Bible the Truth?

"And if God choose to put me through the fire,
I hope He understand I couldn't live as a liar!"

—Lesbian Rapper FELONi

Do you believe in the Bible? What does it mean when a person asks, "Do you believe in the Bible?" Are they asking if you believe in every word written within its pages or the general truth that the Bible supposedly espouses? Most of us would say affirmatively that we do believe in the Bible, but guess what? Most of us have never read the Bible from cover to cover! The truth to understanding homosexuality lies in our belief in what the Bible supposedly teaches about homosexuality. In our Judeo-Christian understanding, we are told that the Bible condemns homosexuality and then given some rather spurious examples of God's condemnation of gay people. In truth, we have not thoroughly investigated the evidence. We have relied on our preachers and pastors to inform us what the Bible has to say. We have relied on them to spout their ethnocentric, misogynistic and homophobic biases, which they have been predisposed to when they were young and ignorant. Our preachers have taught us the story of Sodom and Gomorrah. We came away believing that God doesn't like faggots! This story is the foundation of homophobia and the root of a 3,000-year-old conspiracy against same-sex unions. But if you keep reading you're going to find out that we've been taught a lie.

In matters of religion, Judaism is the originator of homophobia. Judaism is the mother of homophobia. Christianity and Islam are her bastard children who merely upchuck (vomit) the lie. Christianity and Islam are simply plagiarists of Jewish teachings. All of these religionists have got it wrong! And when I say "religionists," I'm speaking to Jews, Hebrew Israelites, Christians, Muslims and any other "sect," "group," "cult," "way of life," "belief system," or "nationality" where a "god" is at the center of its belief. A theocracy. Call "it" the Higher Power,

God, Lord, Yahweh, Jehovah, Allah, Buddha, or Jesus ... you are a religionist, no matter how much you fancy yourself removed from "religion." Your "way of life" is a religion if a "god" is at its center!

In the Christian four Gospels (Matthew, Mark, Luke and John) where Jesus specifically/supposedly speaks, we find no condemnation of homosexuality. Jesus "supposedly" stands mute (silent) on the homosexual question—or so we think! And since Jesus left no concrete theology for his people to practice, we can only speculate on what Jesus' view of homosexuality might have been. With some amount of certainty, my reading of Jesus is that he would've been cool with homosexuals because, like everything else in Jewish law, he flip-the-script (went in the opposite direction). The law said, *"Eye for an eye"* and Jesus said, *"Turn the other cheek."* The law said, *"Hate thy enemy"* and he said, *"Love thy enemy."* He was infamous for saying, *"You have heard them say.... But I say unto you ... "* (Matthew 5). Jesus was that brotha who didn't give a damn about what others thought of him! His whole agenda was about turning a deaf ear to the religio-political powers that be. When the religious men of his day stepped to him with so-called hard religious questions, Jesus gave them the middle-finger by writing on the ground (a 1st century way of saying, *"Fuck you! I ain't tryna hear alla dat!"*) (John 8:6). Oh, Jesus was one bad mutha/shut yo' mouth! ... I'm just talkin' about Jesus! Jesus hung out with prostitutes, an ex-psychopathic crazy woman (Mary Magdalene), militant Malcolm X-type thugs (Zealots) and was thought to be a "winebibber" (an alcoholic) and a glutton (a fat pig!) (Matthew 11:19) There's nothing remotely written in the four Gospels that would lead the reader to suggest that Jesus would have dissed a gay person! Find it! He was so understanding that he even freed the straight woman from her sin of adultery!

And then, Jesus, in all of his wisdom, when making reference to Sodom and Gomorrah (the foundation story of the homophobic myth) talked about how disrespectful and inhospitable those people where (Matthew 10:1-15). Never once did he say anything about their sexual practices!

Christianity's prohibition against homosexuality is the work of one man—Paul. It is he whom addresses the issue of homosexuality, writing:

> For this cause God gave them up unto vile affections: for even their women did exchange the natural use into that which is against nature: and likewise also the men, leaving the natural use of the woman, burned in their lust one toward another; men with men working that which is unseemly ... (Romans 1:26-27).

This, they call Christian "proof" that God hates faggots and dykes! But what the Christian preacher doesn't tell you (out of ignorance or otherwise) is that this scripture has nothing to do with homosexuality! There is no word for homosexuality in the Greek language, the language of the original New Testament. Paul's commentary was a prohibition against so-called idolatrous "cult prostitution," which, in reality, was not prostitution as we understand prostitution, but rather the Roman and Greek religions of Paul's day which used sex as a form of devotion to the Deity (God). He was warning the converted Christians about practicing what he considered pagan religions. Don't worry! I'll delve more into this subject in the last chapter and lay this shyt to rest! Romans 1 is taken out of its historical context and used to teach that God condemns homosexuality. But the reality of the book of ROMANS is that this isn't God's words! This is Paul's words! Who made Paul an authority on God's word? I'll tell you! He did! And we've cosigned all of his lunatic rantings. Do you really think that the Jesus of history would have cosigned a book with the title of his countrymen's oppressor—Rome, Romans? Without Paul's letters (books), the New Testament would be like that empty carton of milk poured over a big-ass bowl of cereal in Ice Cube's movie *Friday*. EMPTY! It is Paul, not Jesus who formulates the Christian doctrine. The religion should be called "Paulanity."

No Christian has the balls to question Paul and his teachings! But Paul is a deceiver! Nowhere in the Old Testament (the first 39 books of the Protestant Bible) do you find a condemnation of two women bumpin' uglies (lesbianism). **The Interpreter's Dictionary of the Bible** (the Rolls Royce of Bible dictionaries) writes, *"Lesbianism is not mentioned in the O.T. [Old Testament], but is condemned in the N.T. [New Testament]"* (Supplemental Volume, Crim et al., p. 819). So I challenge you to read my book, **Ghetto Religiosity II: Uncovering the Naked Truth**, the chapter, **"Saul, Paul ... You Ain't Right!"** where I *break him off something real proper like* and expose him as an uncle-Tom, snitching, murderous, traitor, quisling, puppet, hireling, lackey, satrap dog of Rome! Paul's writings are indeed anti-gay! But they are also anti-Semitic, anti-marriage, and anti-heterosexual unions! Paul, not Jesus, is the one who picks up the homophobic mantle! In fact, Paul, a man who never met the physical or resurrected Christ, has more to say about the Christian faith than Jesus! He is the one who names the faith "Christianity!" (Acts 11:26). This is the reason we have to ask, *"Is the Bible the Truth?"* The Bible has been in the hands of wicked men! Just because a man (Paul) claims to have had a *"vision on the road to Damascus"* doesn't mean that we have to wholeheartedly accept his revelation as divinely revealed truth. What is certain about Paul (from his own mouth) is that he was a Christian persecutor, jailer and murderer of his own countrymen! (Acts 22:4) This we know! His claim to have seen a "spirit Jesus" in the sky is a little—how should I put this?—suspicious! Paul's writings against homosexuality can only be "authoritative" to those of you who accept his revelation/writings. But for the author, he's a fraud, masquerading as a prophet. He is a man who has misrepresented the historical Jesus and the Risen Christ and his teachings. Like the philosopher Voltaire who claimed that Paul's persecution of the Jews was based on his rejection by the daughter of his pharisaic teacher Gamliel, which caused him to become a scorned man and a persecutor of those of "That Way" (Jewish Christians) and Nietzsche, who wrote that *"The 'God' whom Paul invented, a god who ruins the wisdom of the world … To consider Paul … honest when he dresses up hallucination as proof that the Redeemer still lives … What he himself did not believe, the idiots among whom he threw his doctrine believed"* (Kaufmann 618). Paul was the first "SLIM SHADY!" All of his books are suspect! He is not to be believed!

For many of you reading this, questioning the validity of the apostle Paul and the Bible are tantamount to blaspheming God's Name. Many of you may be shocked and even consider me an atheist. Cool. All of your life you've heard and read about Paul and his preaching and then here comes a hip-hop head telling you that Paul is a fraud—and expecting you to believe his word! Trust me when I tell you that my accusations against Paul and the Bible are not the vain "opinions" of a uniformed disbeliever. Everything I write about has been researched *ad nauseam.*

Is the Bible a lie? Hell no! The Bible ain't never lied! It's the people who have misinterpreted—the people who have interpolated—flip the script—done historical gymnastics! The Bible is the creation of "inspired" men. But inspiration does not connotate perfection. The Bible is flawed, full of inaccuracies and contradictions. Read my book, ***Ghetto Religiosity 2000: Third Millennium Liberation***, the chapter, ***"Does the Bible Contradict itself?"*** for the particulars and twenty-five scriptural examples where the Bible has erred. So I boldly assert that the Bible has misrepresented homosexuality as sin.

Jesus and Rappers: The Gay "Rap" On The Messengers.

My father never hugged me when I was a child! My father never kissed me as a child! My father never told me he loved me as a child! I wonder where he got his parenting skills. Cultural conditioning. When I became a man and had kids I swore I would shower them with love and an outward show of affection to make up for all of the missed hugs and kisses that I so craved from my father. And I did! I remember, as a father, kissing my son on the lips from birth up until the age of about four and then, one day as I went in for the lip lock, he stopped me cold. *"No daddy! Boys don't kiss on the mouth!"* It happened just like that in one day! I don't know where he got the idea. Cultural conditioning. I obliged him and we never went there again, but I continued to kiss my older daughter on the lips until she was about thirteen—until she realized it was more fun to kiss boys!

Many of you young hip-hop homophobes are trippin' because rappers Weezy F. Baby a.k.a. Lil Wayne and the Birdman a.k.a. Baby like to kiss each other on the mouth. So they're gay huh? That's what most of the Internet gangsta-bloggers say. *"That's fuckin' homo! A nigga kissin' anotha nigga on the lips! Ugh!"*

Hetero hip-hop heads are actually repulsed by their "father-son" show of affection! Well I'm not! Big-ups to them for not continuing the male-posturing stance of "high-fives" and "pounds" when greeting and showing love to one another. In many cultures it is totally acceptable for males to kiss one another on the lips. Some of our fathers still kiss us on the lips and we don't think any fag-gotry is involved. So why we gotta take it there with these two rappers? We don't know the full extent of their relationship! What we do know is that Baby is a "father-figure" to Lil Wayne. What we do know is that both of these rappers have children—by women—through the act of sexual intercourse. What we also know (but many of us won't admit) is that many of us grown-ass men desire to have a father in our lives! Can't we just accept that Lil Wayne has found his father and that their bond is so strong that they don't mind kissing one another on the lips—and phuck what the world thinks? And check it! After all of the fag-bashing, a group of *MTV aficionados* made Lil Wayne their number one pick as the rapper with the most swagger—over Fiddy, TI, Jay-Z, Kanye West, etc.—a man who kissed another man on the mouth! That homo-bashing shyt is played!

Our society is phucked up! Every man has kissed a male on the mouth! It may have been your dad, your uncle, your mama's boyfriend, your son, your male cousin, your older brother or whomever—but a male has kissed you on the mouth! And if you think men kissing men on the mouth is gay, I dare you to tell that to some of these Italian Mafiosos! Those are some real gangsters! Remy Ma and a few other rappers have rapped, *"Gangstas don't dance!"* as though they are real gangstas! Shut the phuck up with that bullshyt! Naw! The "real" gangsters (Italian/Russian Mafias, Asian Triads) don't make music! These gangsters kill! Have they not seen *The Godfather*, parts I, II, III and *Scarface*? Gangsters do dance! Do they not remember in *The Godfather* how Marlon Brando danced with his wife and daughter at his daughter's wedding and later on with his grandson? Do they not remember the scene where *Tony Montana*/Al Pacino dances with his boss's wife in *Scarface*? How does dancing make you less gangsta? How does a sacred kiss of loyalty and love between two men make them less manly or homosexual? I'm just sayin' …

It would mean something entirely different if these rappers were inserting a tongue in each other's mouths! Then you could make a case that they were gay. But as the argument stands, you could make a case that a man who kisses his mother on the lips is doing an incestuous thing. Or an adult who kisses a child on the lips is a pedophile. Or a pet owner who kisses his dog on the mouth is into bestiality! Now isn't that nonsense? Of course it is! This is what we have done with Lil Wayne and Baby—made a "mountain out of a molehill!" They're laughing at the shock-value of it all.

Unlike the Madonna-Britney Spears-Christina Aguilera French-kiss at the *VMA's* a few years back, Wayne and Baby don't insert tongue into mouth. And what did every HETOERSEXUAL man in America think about the ménage-a-trois kiss? We loved that shyt! We love lesbian sex! We wanted more! We wanted to see Madonna whip out a dildo and fuck the shyt out of those two young impressionable white chicks! Yes we did! Homosexual sex between two women and a man is the all-American male fantasy, yet we are repulsed by two brothas exchanging a gentlemanly kiss of respect. Can you say HYPOCRITE?

Lil Wayne and Baby are actually making a bold statement about manhood and what it means to have brotherly/fatherly-son love. Truth be told, they are very in line with the "Jesus Tradition" of men who show outward affection for other men, without the stigma of homosexuality. It is a very First Century Christian thing for men to kiss on the mouth. Men, in ancient times were very affectionate towards one another. Men kissed, hugged, held hands and even lounged in each other's arms/chest while sitting.

We've all heard of Jesus and the "Last Supper" right? We are taught through Christianity that Jesus loves everybody right? So if I were to tell you that Jesus had a "special" love for a person—would that offend you? Would it offend you if I told you that Jesus' "special friend" was a "young man?" Would it really get your goat going if I told you that some religious scholars have questioned that relationship with this young man and made some homosexual references and inferences? Would you wanna kick my butt if I showed you in the Bible that Jesus and this "beloved disciple" or "young man" were quite cozy, lying in each other's arms? Would it startle you that the Bible makes reference to this young man as *"cloth cast about his naked body"*? Would you totally wanna burn this book if I told you that there was a group of early Christians that called into question Jesus' sexuality and that a certain Christian leader was so outraged by their interpretation that he ordered part of the Biblical scriptures expunged (removed) from your Bible?

Now before you get it twisted, I'm not calling Jesus gay. I'm simply letting all of you heterosexual, Christian, homophobic hypocrites know that Jesus suffered from a First Century *"Weezy F. Baby Syndrome."* The same shyt that many in the heterosexual hip-hop community are accusing Lil Wayne and Baby of—being gay, your man Jesus faced similar accusations in Christian history. Peep this scene from the Last Supper:

> ... Verily, verily [truly, truly], I say unto you, that one of you shall betray [snitch on] me ... **Now there was leaning on Jesus' bosom [chest] one of his disciples, whom Jesus loved ... He then lying on Jesus' breast** saith unto him, who is it? (St. John 13:23-25)

See? What do you make of these scriptures? One of Jesus' disciples was lounging in his arms! If we caught Lil Wayne lying in Baby's chest, we would have a conniption fit! Our society does not permit men to show affection in this manner. But here was Jesus and his "beloved disciple" intimately lounging in a position that most of us Twenty-first century homophobes would deem as GAY! But oh we say we love Jesus, as we floss our blinged-out Jesus pieces and crosses around our necks. We can accept the written word of the Bible but we can't accept the application of Jesus' actions in our own time. Could Jesus get away with this show of affection today—genuine affection between two men with no sexual connotation? If you saw Baby and Weezy in this position you would swear they had to be gay! And I say, if they are gay, then so was Jesus!

And notice too—why does this scripture say in reference to this disciple, *"whom Jesus loved?"* Doesn't that seem odd, peculiar or even queer? Does not Jesus love ALL OF HIS DISCIPLES? Does not our Christianity teach that Jesus loves EVERYBODY? If I have twelve friends and I have to point out a specific one by saying "the one I love," by inference, implication, extrapolation, and common sense a reasonable person would conclude that their relationship was exceptionally different from the other eleven. That ain't hard to see! The case can be made that Jesus had a "special love" for this particular disciple, and indeed he did! Could Jesus possibly have had a homosexual relationship on the D/L with this "Beloved Disciple?" Hold that thought.

Check out the scene after they arrested Jesus!

> And there followed him [Jesus] *a certain YOUNG MAN, having linen cloth cast about his NAKED BODY;* and the young men laid hold on him, And he left the linen cloth and ran *NAKED* (St. Mark 14:51-52).

Hmmm? Why does the Bible want us to know that this young man was naked—twice? Some scholars have identified this young man as Lazarus or John (but that is insignificant to this essay). The point is that Jesus had a "special" relationship with this young man, just as Baby has a "special" relationship with Lil Wayne. You can call Lil Wayne and Baby gay, but I bet you're scared as shyt to make that comparison to Jesus, so let me make it for you! Again, I'll say that if Lil Wayne and Baby are gay, then so were Jesus and this young man!

This isn't the end of Jesus' love for this young man! Peep game! After Jesus is resurrected what happens? Read!

> Then she [Mary Magdalene] runneth, and cometh to Simon Peter, and to the *OTHER DISCIPLE, WHO JESUS LOVED*, and saith unto them ... (St. John 20:2)

What? *"The other disciple, whom Jesus loved?"* What the hell does that mean? Again, does not Jesus love ALL of the disciples? Why then would the Bible say, *"Peter and to the other disciple, whom Jesus loved?"* Why not, *"Peter and the other disciple?"* Or, *"Jesus' beloved disciples, Peter and Lazarus?"* Why does the Bible want us to know that Jesus' love for one young man was different than that of Peter and the rest of the disciples?

Some of y'all might think I'm reading too much into the way it was written, so let's change the names! *"Then she runneth, and cometh unto Simon Peter and to*

Lil Wayne, whom Baby loved. "Now you see the problem! If Jesus was "Baby" and Mary was "Trina" and the Other Disciple was "Lil Wayne" … you get the picture!

Did you forget that when they came to arrest Jesus, Judas kissed him? (Matthew 26:47-49) Does this make Jesus and Judas gay? I think not! But reading the Internet bloggers, any man who kisses another man in the mouth has got to be gay! The Bible does not say where Judas kissed Jesus. It could've been on his cheek, forehead or lips. Whichever way it went down, it would not be interpreted as homosexuality back then.

Again, sometimes a kiss can just be a kiss! Our culture dictates that a man shouldn't kiss another man on the lips. But what's so wrong with it, whether homosexual or heterosexual?

Ya boy Jesus was very in tune with what we today call his "feminine side." The Bible even portrays Jesus in a very androgynous (male/female) way. In the book of Revelations 1:13 it describes Jesus as dressed with a *"girt about the paps with a golden girdle."* Do you know what "paps" are? Paps are breasts and nipples! Do you know what a "girdle is? A girdle is a band or belt that holds the mid-section in place—like something your mama might wear to tuck in her gut.

If Jesus came back today he'd look like a first century version of Prince! And just like many of you homophobes think that Prince is gay because of his eccentric appearance (arched eyebrows and androgynous visage) and high heel shoes, so it was with Jesus. If you knew the real historical Jesus you wouldn't be a homophobe because Jesus was that "faggot-looking/acting" dude in first century Palestine by today's standards. What am I talking about? Number one! The Gospels (Matthew, Mark, Luke, and John) never, ever … never ever ever … make mention of his sex life—with a man or a woman! A dude that ain't fuckin' today is either gay or asexual—or so we believe. And then the brotha (Jesus) was hanging out 24/7 with twelve MEN! A 1st Century DMX could've rapped, *"I love my bytches, but where my niggas?"* We have the advantage of hindsight and understanding through centuries of Christian brainwashing that Jesus had a spiritual message, but put yourself back in that time. Come on now! And then we read through religious history about a disturbing story of Jesus and a young man engaged in some ultra-secretive sexual/initiation rite. What? Yes! There's a set of scriptures that were so disturbing to one early church father that he had them removed from the Bible because of its implied sexual innuendo. You've already read the remnants of Jesus and his *"beloved disciple,"* or *"the one whom Jesus loved."* Those are the fragments of a larger untold story that the Bible editors were careless about getting rid of the evidence. They never foresaw a day when the masses could actually read, write and think critically about religious issues. But here we are! Now check it! Here's what's left out of your Bible regarding the relationship between the *"one whom Jesus loved"* and himself. Mark 10 (somewhere between verses 34-35) used to read like this:

> *"And they come into Bethany. And a certain woman whose brother had died was there. And, coming, she prostrated herself before Jesus and says to him, 'Son of David, have mercy on me.' But the disciples rebuked her. And Jesus, being angered, went off with her into the garden where the tomb was, and straightway a great cry was heard from the tomb. And going near, Jesus rolled away the stone from the door of the tomb. And straightaway, going in where the youth was, he stretched forth his hand and raised him, seizing his hand. **But the youth, looking upon him, loved him and began to beseech him that he might be with him**. And going out of the tomb, they came into the house of the youth, for he was rich. And after six days Jesus told him what to do, and in the evening **the youth comes to him, wearing a linen cloth over his naked body. And he remained with him that night,** for Jesus taught him the mystery of the Kingdom of God. And thence, arising, he returned to the other side of the Jordan."*

These scriptures are referred to by religious historians/scholars as *"The Secret Gospel of Mark."* They were found by Professor Morton Smith in 1958, southeast of Jerusalem. It is Professor Morton Smith that puts forth the theory that Jesus was a homosexual and he and this young man were doin' the do. Why was it removed from the Gospel of Mark in you Bible? You see, after Jesus died, there were many interpretations of his message that arose. The Christian faith was not monolithic (one minded) in its infancy. There were many schools of thought concerning Jesus and his teachings. By the end of the first century A.D./C.E. there arose groups of Christians called "Gnostics" (pronounced "nostics"). The word Gnostic means "knowledge." They professed to have secret/esoteric knowledge about the teachings of Yahshua Hammashiah (Jesus Christ). By the fourth century, these so-called "heretic" Gnostic Christians were made an anathema ... a pariah (religious outcasts), leading up to Emperor Constantine's "quasi/pseudo" conversation to Christianity, thus unifying, codifying and harmonizing the Christian faith as one monolithic voice, culminating at the famous Council of Nicaea in 325 A.D. This is what your church doesn't teach you concerning Christianity's rise to becoming a world religion. A lot of bullshyt went down between the death of Jesus and the fourth century world council at Nicaea. There was even a great school of thought called "Arianism" that challenged Jesus' divinity! It took 400 years to work out the particulars of the Christian faith. The

Council of Nicaea solidified Jesus' divinity as *"consubstantial with the Father,"* meaning *"of the same substance."* Jesus was pronounced *"Very God."*

But prior to this event a group of Gnostics called "Carpocratians" taught the above scriptures and they interpreted them as a homosexual religious initiation rite. According to the Carpocratians, their text of Mark contained the phrase "**gymnon gymno**," which translates as "**naked man with naked man**." Ooooh! Clement was hot about it! This angered Clement of Alexander to the point that he had to write a letter, warning of the vile teachings of the Gnostic Carpocratians. And guess what? We have the letter! Wanna read it? Here it goes! To Theodore:

> You did well in silencing the unspeakable teachings of the Carpocratians. For these are the *"wandering stars"* referred to in the prophecy, who wander from the narrow road of the commandments into a boundless abyss of the carnal and bodily sins. For, priding themselves in knowledge, as they say, *"of the deep things of Satan"*, they do not know that they are casting themselves away into *"the nether world of the darkness"* of falsity, and boasting that they are free, they have become slaves of servile desires. Such men are to be opposed in all ways and altogether. For, **even if they should say something true, one who loves the truth should not, even so, agree with them. For not all true things are the truth, ...** To them, therefore, as I said above, one must never give way; nor, when they put forward their falsifications, should **one concede that the secret Gospel is by Mark, but should even deny it on oath. For, *"Not all true things are to be said to all men"***

Maaan! There are subtle implications that the Carpocratians indeed speak the truth! *"... not all true things are to be said to all men ... "* This is why you have the Knights Templars, the Freemasons, the Eastern Stars, the Shriners, the Rosicrucians, the Jesuits, the Illuminati, the Skull & Bones, the Bilderburg Group, the Trilateral Commission, the Council on Foreign Relations, the Priory of Sion, etc.—and even college fraternities and sororities are founded on initiation rituals (hazing, crossing the burning sands) and secrecy. Humankind, for the last 2,000 years have invested in hording knowledge. There is a belief that some things are best kept secret! That's the premise of the whole *The Da Vinci Code* hoopla. Could the "Holy Grail" have actually been the womb of Mary Magdalene, which was to carry the bloodline of Jesus? Again, *"not all true things are to be said to all men."* Or as Jack Nicholson would say, *"You want the truth? You can't handle the truth!"* Hell! Right here in our own time our government won't come clean about the Roswell UFO crash (1947) and Area 51! Our government chooses to think for us! They don't think we can handle knowing that there is life beyond out little puny planet and that their intelligence is light years ahead of ours! As it relates to religious matters, there's a whole lot of shyt that the learned men take as matter-of-factly, but keep to themselves, such as the stuff you've just read about the Secret Gospel of Mark! This ain't no new teaching! It is the "skeletons-in-the-closet," which all religions harbor. The history of Christianity, like Judaism and Islam is wrought with violence and murder—from the Spanish Inquisition to the African "hellocaust" to the Jewish holocaust—Christianity has been a muth-afucka on humanity!

The Secret Gospel of Mark is part of the controversy of Christianity. Was Jesus Gay? Did Jesus have sex with this young man? We'll never know for sure but isn't it interesting to read the controversies surrounding the advent of Christianity? Some say Lil Wayne and Baby are gay. Some said that Jesus was gay. It's the gay "rap" on the messengers.

And just to give a fair and balance view of the Jesus of history (unlike ortho-dox Christianity, which teaches an "asexual"/without sex Jesus), there were other Gnostic texts such had the Gospel of Philip, which presumes Jesus to be a VERY SEXUAL person, kissing the likes of Mary Magdalene to the point of making the other disciples angry and jealous. Here's an excerpt.

> And the companion of the Savior is Mary Magdalene. But Christ loved her more than all the disciples and used to kiss her often on the mouth. The rest of the disciples were offended by it and expressed disapproval. They said unto him, *"Why do you love her more than all of us?"* The Savior answered and said unto them, *"Why do I not love you like her?"*

WOW! See? On the one hand many Christians are angered and repulsed by me mentioning the Secret Gospel of Mark, where Jesus and a young man were supposedly involved in some type of sexual/ritualistic man love. How dare the author insinuate that Jesus was gay! And then I show where Jesus was straight and sticking his tongue all down Mary Magdalene's throat and again, they are repulsed that Jesus was a sexual creature—kissing—and by extrapola-tion—phucking! So, my dear Christians, you make the call! Do you wanna believe in the mythologized Christ of institutional Christianity or the historical/human Yahshua (Jesus) of 2,000 years ago?

Niggas Be Holdin' Them Dicks!—Richard Pryor

Public displays of affection are very common among the ancients. Yes! Men kissed each other in biblical times. I'll even go a step further and tell you that men swore by and on their dicks—that men held other men's penises when performing an oath! What? You don't believe me? Okay. What do you make of these scriptures?

> And Abraham said unto his eldest servant of his house … Put, I pray thee, thy hand under my **"thigh"**: And I will make thee swear by the Lord … and the servant put his hand under the **"thigh"** of Abraham his master, and swear to him … (Genesis 24: 2-3 & 9)

> And the time drew nigh that Israel [Jacob] must die: and he called his son Joseph, and said unto him, If now I have found grace in thy sight, put, I pray thee, thy hand under my **"thigh,"** and deal kindly and truly with me (promise/swear me your oath) … And he said, Swear unto me … (Genesis 47: 29 & 31)

> … uncover thy locks, make bare the leg, uncover the **"thigh"** … Thy nakedness shall be uncovered; yea thy shame shall be seen … (Isaiah 47:2-3)

Notice the word "thigh?" Does thigh mean the upper portion of a person's leg? No! Not in the biblical sense. "Thigh" is a EUPHEMISM (nice language) for a man's dick, penis, prick, Johnson, or cock! And back in biblical times men touched one another on their dicks and made vows, promises, and oaths!—So-called straight, religious men! Abraham! Jacob! Touched dicks! **The Eerdmans Bible Dictionary** defines "thigh" as:

> The proximity of the thigh to the genitals allows the word to be a euphemism for "genitals" [sex organs]. The placing of one's hand under a person's thigh—i.e., touching the genitals, the seat of life—in the course of swearing an oath places one into contact with the life-force (i.e. the procreative powers) of the other person and so underlines the seriousness of the oath (Myers et. al, pg. 999).

See? I didn't manufacture this shyt! That's how they were living back then! Could you imagine (as a straight man) grabbing another man's dick and saying, *"Word to my mother playa!"*? Rappers love to hold their dicks when they rhyme! Richard Pryor joked, *"Niggas be holdin' them dicks!"* Now we see that men have been holding dicks for three millenniums!

Things aren't always as they appear! Jesus was no more "gayer" than Abraham, Jacob, Baby and Lil Wayne! The problem is that our minds have been conditioned to accept and reject certain ideas of manhood and heterosexuality and anything that is outside of our perception of masculinity is deemed homo. In reality, all heterosexual men are "homo"! As the previous chapter explained, "homo" sim- ply means "man" and "same." Jesus was homo! Baby and Lil Wayne are homos—"men" of the "same" mindset. I'm a homo! Every Internet blogger who says, *"No homo here!"* is a homo!—and an ignorant homo at that! You might not suck a dick, but everything else about you is homo! Your mannerisms—HOMO! (same) Your dress—HOMO! (same) Prince and Michael Jackson are the most HETERO men we've ever seen! Why? Because their mannerisms and dress are nothing like our so-called heterosexualism! "Hetero" means "different" and "opposite." They definitely dress "different" and "opposite" of most men. You ever seen Prince rockin' an oversized white T-shirt, an iced-out Jesus piece, some *Red Monkey* jeans, a fitted baseball cap and some Uptowns (*Nikes*)? Hell No! You ever seen Michael Jackson dressed in a three-quarter length business suit (minus the epaulettes and medals of nothing) and a Godfather brim with gators to match? It ain't gonna happen! The only tennis shoes we've ever seen Michael Jackson in were some very feminine-looking black buckles & rhinestone *L.A. Gears!* (Circa 1990). And he wasn't even playing basketball! He was dancing on a darkened street, doing the *Running Man* and ghetto pirouettes! Those shoes were so unmanly. If a nicca stepped on the court with them shyts on, he'd be the last picked and talked about from here to eternity! But don't front! Some of us rocked them! Some of our mamas put them on their children—who grew up to be gang- sta rappers! (lol!) This is our heterocentric culture.

Why Gay Hip-Hop/Rap?

○ ○

*"Hip-hop's one of the most homophobic of all musical genres ...
There's an excitability in our culture around issues like homosexuality, transvestites and so on. And as wonderful and outrageous and
avant garde as rap is, it's never meaningfully challenged any of these
boundaries ... the hip-hop community isn't suddenly going to
embrace these folk [gays/lesbians], but they're going to have to make
their peace with them one way or another."*

—Professor Michael Eric Dyson
(Author of Holler If You Hear Me: Searching for Tupac Shakur)

First of all, why not? We've got gangsta rap (Just Ice/NWA/Snoop Dogg/The
Game), beefing rap (50 Cent/Ja Rule), freaknik rap (Two-Live Crew/Petey
Pablo), party rap (Hammer/Young Joc) dope boy rap (Young Jezzy/Rick Ross),
sex rap (Trina/Lil Kim), backpack rap (A Tribe Called Quest/Kanye West), conscious rap (Common/Talib Kweli), militant rap (Public Enemy/dead prez). And
then there's Snap, Crunk, and Hyphy rap genres. So what's the problem with gay
rap, besides homophobia? You homophobic hip-hop rap niggas sound just like
white folks sounded forty years ago when the day came for integration and they
had to "allow" black folk to eat in the same restaurant and drink out of the same
water fountain and shit in the same toilet! Listen to yourselves! They thought that
our black skin was gonna rub off on them or we got some different kind of germs
that were unheard of in white people. Some of y'all think there's a "gay" germ or
you're gonna turn gay or someone might mistaken you for gay. You're just as
hypocritical and bigoted as a 1950's Southern racist cracka—ass cracka! (Chris
Rock's expression) They used to call white people who helped blacks achieve civil
rights "nigger lovers." So, by all means, call me "faggot lover." I'll be dat!

There might come a day when these so-called "faggots" start physically fighting back against homophobia. "Gayngsta" rapper Deadlee alludes to that when

he raps, *[You heterosexuals]* *"Dissin' faggots blindly, I'm doin' you the same! [to you heterosexuals] Unless you change the rules in this fucked-up rap game. Realest nigga after 50 Cent, you lookin' tame. Homo-thug for life G-A-Y-N-G ... bang! Crucified for the truth, like Jesus I will hang. When the faggots strike back, I will take the blame. Sunday, bloody Sunday, they killin' in my name. Spell it! D-E-A-D-L-E-E ... for all the years of shame!"*

Sounds like there ain't gonna be too much more name-calling without repercussions! Brothas will fuck you up for talking about their mama! Deadlee is warning us that the day will come when a homosexual goes over the deep end and pulls a "Columbine" or a "Virginia Tech" for being teased about his or her homosexuality. And just as others claim to have killed in the name of Marilyn Manson, some psychotic homosexual might take Deadlee's lyrics literally and take matters into his own hands. Better give ear to the prophet! There is a great amount of anger brewing in the homosexual community, listening to these lyrics. We don't hear him though!

We, hip-hop heterosexual males think we're the baddest S.O.B.'s walking the earth! We think we can't be touched—especially by some gay dude. Oh hell no! We've learned nothing from the deaths of Tupac, Biggie, Big L, Jam Master Jay, Soldier Slim, Freaky Tah, Mac Dre, Proof, Big Hawk, Izzy Ramirez, Philant Johnson and Stack Bundles. Black men are dying all over America over some bullshit! We're still beefing over bullshit! Many black men don't give a damn about the next black man, so you know they give less than two shits about a homosexual man. *"Effin' faggot! Eat a dick!"* We're comfortable in our homophobia, so much so, that we freely use the words homo and fag on our rap albums. But I must say that nobody is more homophobic than some of our West Indian (Island) brothers. Jamaican reggae stars, in particular, seem to have a fixation with homosexuality—yea, a goddamned cultural/nationalistic unwritten duty to call for homosexuals to die a violent death! They are utterly absorbed, consumed and immersed in singing violent diatribes against homosexuals! They make songs that specifically address homosexuals! It is of the greatest importance that they let the rest of their people know that homosexuality is evil and should be wiped off the earth. They call homosexual men "chi chi men" and "batty boys," meaning bottom/lying-on-your-back-like-a-woman boys. Beanie Man, Elephant Man, Sizzla, T.O.K., Buju Banton and Bounty Killer—these brothas take homophobia into another realm! And while some of them have signed a "pact" not to sing homophobic songs, none of them have publicly denounced their own homophobic lyrics or reggae's homophobia.

A distinct difference can be made between American rappers' homophobia and some reggae stars' homophobia—rappers mostly use "fag" as slang to debase another rapper's lyrical acuity. "Fag" in rap terms, usually means "soft," and "lyrically weak." Generally speaking, it has nothing to do with debasing a homosexual person, just as a rapper using the word "nigga" as a term of endearment, unlike the wretched "nigger," which is a racist term used to debase a whole people. Unlike some reggae stars, rappers don't make songs addressing homosexuals. That would be *ghey*! The most ghetto-ass hardcore rapper knows just how far to push the fag-bashing envelope. You're not gonna hear a rapper rap about killing a homosexual—that's just unacceptable in our society. Oh, but these backwards-assed Island coons actually call for the death of homosexuals!—and their record companies put out their records! This bleach-blond/yellow/red-haired jigg named Elephant Man, whose video has aired on *B.E.T.* and he's appeared on *106 & Park* raps, *"When you hear lesbians getting raped, it's not our fault. Two women in bed, that's two Sodomites that should be dead! Batty man fi dead/Queers must be killed/Shoot dem like bird!"*

Shame on *B.E.T.*! Fuck how popular they are! If they are out-n-out homophobes, then we should ban them from our media like the Black Plague and send a message to any artist that *that* shit doesn't fly just because you're black. This ain't a censorship issue either! *B.E.T.* would not air a video by a white racist who called for black death in his song. *B.E.T* is hypocritical and a two-faced spineless machine! You air videos by known homophobes, yet the minute a Jewish voice is raised in criticism of a Michael Jackson lyric, you pull the plug on his video, as not to offend Jews! *"Jew me, sue me, kick me, kike me!"* What the fuck is that compared to *"kill a batty bwoy?"*

Bounty Killer raps, *"Mister faggoty, wince in agony!"* Meanwhile, your country is reminiscent of a Third World Whorehouse, yet you have the time to rhyme violent diatribes against your fellow gay and lesbian countrymen? You scream, *"Jah Rastafari!"* and wish that homosexuals be raped and killed? Rastafarianism is a beautiful "way of life" that preaches love, respect, justice, unity and freedom from oppression—yet you oppress some of your own people because of their sexual orientation? That makes you and/or your understanding of religion hypocritical. You claim that Emperor Haile Selassie was the *"Conquering Lion of the Tribe of Judah"*—that he was Jesus revisited—the messiah—a man whom many Jamaicans and others have adopted as Savior—a man who was not a Rastafarian and didn't advocate this religion and did not see himself as a holy figure. Yet you can't find one speech or quote where Selassie puts gays and lesbians down or preached death to the batty bwoy! That homophobic shit coming from the Islands is not

Rastafarianism! It is cultural imperialism masquerading as religious truth! Haile Selassie encouraged freedom and tolerance! He said:

> "Since nobody can interfere in the realm of God, we should tolerate and live side by side with those of other faiths.... We wish to recall here the spirit of tolerance shown by our Lord Jesus Christ when he gave forgiveness to all, including those that crucified him." ... "Throughout history, it has been the inaction of those who could have acted, the indifference of those who should have known better, the silence of the voice of justice when it mattered most that has made it possible for evil to triumph."

And this freedom and tolerance went beyond the religious realm. That was his life's work! You may have been raised to hate gay people in the Islands, but it is wrong! Raise up your voices in song and proclaim that it is evil to sing praise to the raping and murdering of homosexual people! Admit it! Most of you Island niggas ain't studied the Bible and found homosexuality to be a sin against God! You're just parroting some cultural garbage passed down from one ignorant Third World generation to another! Your understanding of homosexuality is crude and unsophisticated. You see the word "herb" in the Bible and you ignorantly interpret that as smoking ganja, spliffs, marijuana! Why don't you smoke collard greens or lettuce? Can you say EXEGETICS? That's how you study the Bible! This is God-talk!

It ain't gay people who got your ass living in shantytowns! It's your goddamned Colonial/quasi-BLACK government that's got you livin' in hell! Don't hate! Respect the truth! And the truth is that a gay Reggaeton, Dance Hall or Reggae artist will emerge from the islands and shut some of this homophobic ignorance down! Ire mon!

Eminem rivals these Third World Island fucks when he raps, *"My words are like a dagger with a jagged edge. That'll stab you in the head. Whether you're a fag or lez. Or the homosex, hermaph or trans-a-vest. Pants or dress—hate fags? The answer is yes!"* But a gay rapper named Dutchboy challenges Eminem's definition of "fag" with a superb retort when he raps, *"They say a fag is a feminine actin' guy, but to me it's anybody got somethin' to hide.... Eminem is a faggot for braggin' on beatin' his wife. Every fake ass rapper is just a fag with a mic. Always lookin' for the lesser one to fuck with. That's a bitch move! You just another spoil rich dude!"* You're telling me that these homo-rappers ain't got nothin' relevant to say? Heteros please! Bring on gay hip-hop!

I find it quite insulting to even ask such an asinine and insidious question about gays in hip-hop! Hell, why hip-hop at all? What is hip-hop if it is not all-inclusive of anyone who's got something relevant to say? Detroit lesbian rapper FELONi sees the hypocrisy and contradiction in hetero-mainstream hip-hop/rap and asks the very poignant question when she raps, *"If hip-hop is here to* **represent** *the* **black collective***, then what the fuck is it about* **MY black perspective***?"* Very profound indeed! She's asking, "Why am I shut out of the mainstream? Because I'm lesbian?" It's not like every straight rapper is droppin' science when they open their mouths. Quite the contrary and so much so that Nas declared, *"Hip-hop is dead!"*

Hip-hop was born out of poverty—out of powerlessness—out of voiceless-ness. When N.W.A. came on the scene, no one asked, "Why gangsta rap?" And if they did, it didn't matter. Gangsta rap didn't give a fuck about what mainstream America (or other genres of rap) thought about its misogynistic and gangster lyr-ics. When "Freaknic rap" (as rapped by the likes of Two-Live Crew) came on the scene, there wasn't a backlash from within the hip-hop community over the way they portrayed women. The government may have had problems with what they were rapping about but they couldn't stop that Freedom of Speech train they were riding.

So, I ask, "Why not gay hip-hop?" If ... if ... if gay Liberace can prance around in diamonds and furs and let his well-manicured fingers stroke the keys of the piano playing CLASSICAL music and sell millions of records and sell out Vegas—If gay Little Richard, the self-proclaimed "Architect of ROCK & ROLL" can woo black and white audiences with *Tutti Fruiti* and *Long Tall Sally* all the way to the bank—If gay Freddy Mercury and Queen can sing *We Are The Cham-pions* and *Bohemian Rhapsody* (arguably one of the greatest rock songs ever) and still not damage the persona of ROCK—If gay Elton John can be a force in ROCK, POP and SOUL singing *Bennie and the Jets*—If gay Sylvester can sing DISCO and have all the straight bell-bottom wearing men doing the bump—If gay gender-bending Boy George can wear a face prettier than most women and still garner mainstream attention singing POP—If gay George Michaels can sing R&B and not shame the genre—If gay cross-dressing Rupaul can have a top 40 record on the radio—If Madonna can introduce a record and a dance called *Vogue*, which was created by homosexual men and make it a dance craze—If "ex-gay" Donnie McClurkin can put a Band-Aid (religion) on his (homo)-sexuality and sell millions of GOSPEL records along with feminine-acting Dr. Bobby Jones—then why the phuck can't we have a GAY "gayngsta" Tupac-esque RAP-PER named ***Deadlee***? Why can't we have a gay Hispanic brotha from the Mid-west named ***Bigg Nugg*** or a clean-cut non-threatening gay rapper like ***Tori Fixx*** or some innovative, eclectic and socially conscious gay wordsmiths like ***Tim'm***

West, Juba Kalamka, JBRAP, Soul Nubian, Solas B. Lalgee, Buttaflysoul, Baraka Noel, and *Marcus Rene*, collectively known as *Deep Dickollective*? Or an alley cat rhyme-sayer named *Cat-Eyez*, some Strong Island/Crooklyn brothas like *(Bone) Intell* and *Shorty Roc* or a Dirty South brotha named *Diamon D.I.V.A.* or a Chi-Town pretty-boy named *Johnny Dangerous*? Ever heard of a Tampa lesbian trio named *Yo Majesty*? How about a hardcore homophobic rhyming homo named *El-Don*? Why can't we have a pair dime-piece transgendered/transsexual female rappers like *Foxxjazell* and *Pam Jones* or a white-gay-Jew boy-Eminem-esque rapper from New York named *soce—the elemental wizard* and his UK counterpart—*Q-Boy* or some fire-spitting lesbian sistas like *FELONi, Delacruz, Mz Fontaine, Veto Ali, JenRO,* and *Ricoshade* or a Vanilla Ice-influenced white girl named *White Lesbian Rapper (WLR)* or how about a Latino/Hispanic bisexual group called *Salvimex*? *(By the way, these are real gay, lesbian, bisexual, transgendered "GLBT" rappers that have great stories to tell.)*

Why does homo-hop have to stay as a subculture of a subculture? Let's keep it "historically" real! Gay people have influenced hip-hop no matter how homophobic we are and no matter how we feign ignorance of the homo-paradigm!

In-the-closet gay/flamboyant Liberace was such a brilliant musician and entertainer that many in the hetero rap world are on his jock! Dr. Dre, in his song, *California Love* rapped, *"Diamonds shinin', lookin' like I robbed Liberace...."* Mannie Fresh rapped, *"The ring I got, Liberace want it. He couldn't afford that shit, but I can afford to flaunt it!"* Other straight rappers have paid homage to Liberace through their lyrics—Juvenile, Baby, 50 Cent (*Hustler's Ambition*), Kid Rock (*American Bad Ass*), G-Unit (*Stunt 101*), Eminem (*Criminal*), D12 (*Fight Music*), Big Pun (*It's So Hard*), Lil Wayne (*We Fly High*-remix), Clipse (*Mr. Me Too*), Lil Flip (alias Fliporace), Rugged Intellect (*All Fair*). Don't tell me that gay artists haven't influenced hip-hop! Are rappers the first to make it fashionable to wear excessive jewelry? No! Gay Liberace did! Was Cam'ron the first to wear pink fur? No! Gay Liberace wore furs down to the floor! Rapper/producer Jermaine Dupri said, *"You ain't a balla unless you drive one of these!"* (a Bentley). Liberace drove a tricked-out Rolls Royce! And while it may be true that many rappers were/are influenced by the local pimp's fashion sensibilities (think Bishop Don Magic Juan) or movies such as *Superfly* and *The Mack,* none of these characters can match the outlandishness of Liberace and his musical son, Elton John. Whether consciously or unconsciously, covertly or overtly, Liberace set the standard for stuntin'—an ostentatious show of wealth, celebrity fashion, celebrity clothing lines and excessive jewelry. He is the undisputed bling-bling king—the original stunna! And gay Elton John is the prince of stuntin'. Lil Jon might be in the

Guinness World Book of Records for the biggest pendant, but he's just a copier of something a gay man started before he was born! All of your clothing lines, your pink furs, your virgin chinchilla spreads, your outrageous jewelry, your stunna shades (see Elton John's album covers circa 1972-'74), your ostentatious show of wealth—gay, feminine! I didn't create the paradigm. I'm just showing you where hetero rappers have bitten off their sense of style from—gay men!

And even pop stars like Michael Jackson and Prince are afforded great respect by rappers, even though they are very effeminate and androgynous in their appearance, wearing makeup, eyeliner, high heel shoes, tight suits, permed hair—speaking with the softest, feminine voices. Prince is the most metrosexual/androgynous/feminine "Is he gay?" man there is and he gets a pass from every straight man because he's been linked to some of the finest women on the planet! Hetero men wished they had his *savoir faire* when it comes to the ladies. Prince looks so fine and womanly on that one album cover where he's naked that if he had a pair of tits, I'd hit it! MJ and Prince are not models of machismo and virility, yet you ain't never heard the most hardcore rapper diss them! And while their sexuality has been questioned, it hasn't stopped them from selling millions of albums worldwide. What straight man can deny Prince is not the shyt when he sings *Do Me Baby, International Lover, Adore, The Beautiful Ones* and the whole goddamned *Purple Rain* album? That's straight (and gay) phucking music!

Michael Jackson had the biggest selling album in musical history (1982's *Thriller* sold over 100 million albums worldwide), yet there isn't one piece of "known" pussy that he's ever been in! Name one! Brooke Shields? Hell no! She said he ran from the poonanny! Lisa Marie? That fake-ass TV image makeover marriage/kiss after the child molesting allegations, which he settled out of court, awarding the child a rumored 15 million dollar settlement for something he adamantly and vehemently, denies he did! Shiiit! Lisa Marie claimed they never slept in the same bedroom! And the so-called "mother of his children?" Artificial insemination! He didn't even man-up and phuck that ugly white woman to make his children! They even say those aren't his biological children! Anyone with an eye for genetics knows there's not an ounce of Negro blood in those kids! They ain't mulatto, biracial, quadroon, octoroon or niggaroon! As rapper Deadlee raps, *"Ain't been in pussy since the day of my birth!"*—Michael Jackson ... and you know it's true! The same can be said for one of our greatest musical voices—Luther Vandross! We all have made love to his music, but we ain't ever heard that <u>HE</u> was "makin' love" ... to a woman!

The point is that they are making mainstream music despite their quirky eccentric lifestyles. And there are others in the music industry whose sexuality has been questioned as homosexual, like Freddy Jackson, Queen Latifah, Mc Lyte, Da Brat and Missy Elliot. I'm not saying they are gay/lesbian, but the rumor mill in the 'hood has speculated that they are. And still, there are/were many outwardly gay/lesbians in the music industry, including Janis Joplin, Melissa Etheridge, kd lang, Me'Shell NdegeOcello, Chastity Bono, Nona Hendryx, Grace Jones, Iggy Pop, Johnny Mathis, Joan Baez, etc., etc., etc. But goddamnit! Their sexuality just shouldn't matter! It should be about the music and the message and there's a large part of me that feels stupid for even having to write on this subject to make a case for homo hop!

Niccas tripped out and lost their effin' minds when they saw rappers Baby and Lil Wayne kissing each other on the mouth! *"Dem niggas is ghey! Fuckin' fags man! Homo fo' real yo!"* Yeah, I heard you. I read all of y'all's ignant Internet B/S. But when Madonna French-kissed the shit out of Britney Spears and Christina Aguilera on national TV at the VMA's, we hetero heads wanted more! That's our shit! Women gettin' freak-nasty with each other—WOW! What more can a hetero man ask for? After their kiss with Madonna, Christina said, *"She's a good kisser … she's got very soft lips and there's nothing like kissing a woman."* Britney commented, *"This is something I've dreamt about since I was a little girl. I cannot believe this just happened! I am on a major high right now. I feel really cool."* The fallout? What fallout? Their record sales/popularity? Through the roof! Double standard!

Every genre of music has gay and lesbian artists—from gay classical musical composer Tchaikovsky to blues singing lesbian Ma Rainey. Check your music history pimpin'! And then … and then … and then! Here comes the infant of musical genres … rap music frontin' like a gay person ain't got no place or business in this particular genre of music! Get the fuck outta here with that shit! The same genre of music that talks about the underdog, the impoverished, the voiceless, the disenchanted, the disenfranchised, the marginalized, the 'hood, the ghetto, keepin' it real … the dregs of American society! Yeah, rap music has been around 30 years, but that ain't shit on the world stage of musical history! Humankind has been making music for more than 8,000 years! Can you dig that? Rap is still in the womb of the universal language—music! Rap is in its first trimester and can still be aborted like an unwanted fetus at the murder clinic if we don't get it right! Can you say DISCO? Four hundred years from now, when your favorite rapper is taking a dirt nap (dead), will they know about Rakim, Run DMC, LL Cool J, Public Enemy, Dr. Dre, Jay-Z, Nas, 50 Cent, Common, Tupac, Biggie Smalls, Outkast and Snoop Dogg like we know about Bach, Beethoven, Brahms, Mozart, Tchaikovsky, Liszt, Rachmaninov, Handel, Mendelssohn, Stravinsky, Hayden and Shubert? Four hundred years from now will

Nas' *Illmatic* be as relevant as Handel's *Messiah* is today? Will Rakim's *Follow The Leader* be as compelling as Beethoven's *Fifth Symphony*?

This will be the test of the rap genre! Longevity and universal respect and recognition! Or will rap music find itself being relegated to an obscure footnote in the annals of musical history? This is a question for the gatekeepers/vanguard/aficionados of hip-hop/rap to ponder. Most hip-hop heads can't see that far into the future, so naturally homo-hop is not even considered a relevant discussion in the narrow-minded here-and-now world of heterosexualism. But I'm raising the bar of hip-hop consciousness and treading on uncharted ground, which the most progressive hetero rapper dare not go! From "conscious" Common to "Jesus walking" Kanye West who rapped, *"They say you can rap about anything except for Jesus!"* No! *"You can rap about anything except for homosexuality!"* That would be a more accurate statement about the state of hip-hop! Jesus isn't a taboo subject for rappers! (Think MC Hammer, Tupac, DMX, Rev. Run, Kirk Franklin, DC Talk, Gospel Gangstaz and most rappers who make some reference to Jesus or the Lord on their CDs.)

Do you want rap to last? Then it's got to evolve! And homo rap is a part of its evolution. We gotta keep it movin'! Some stuff will be whack, but that's okay! Creativity breeds the good and the not-so-good. Not all hip-hop heads like all types of rap. Gangsta heads don't like backpack heads! Conscious heads don't like party heads! So what! You ain't gotta like every genre of rap, but EVERY genre of rap has a right to be heard! Even the whack-ass heterosexual rap of a fake-ass Vanilla Ice! Get-in-where-you-fit-in and stop hatin' on what you personally don't like. Hell, if we left it up to some people ALL RAP would be banned—even the shit that you like.

I've heard these hetero hip-hop heads talk about gay rap! Ignorantly, sarcastically, smugly and rhetorically they ask, *"Can these gay rappers even rap? Maybe there's never been a mainstream gay rapper because their raps are garbage!"* as if every hetero rapper on the radio is lyrically gifted! To them I say, *"Have you ever taken the time to listen to any gay or lesbian rapper's CD?"* No! Caushun, perhaps the most visible/famous homo rapper that had his "15 minutes of mainstream fame," getting a little shine on *B.E.T.* is probably most heterosexuals' answer to gay hip-hop. A true flaming fag with limited skills and subject material! He has been exposed as the "Milli Vanilli" of homo-hop. Kimora Lee Simmons (ex-wife of Russell Simmons) signed him to her *Baby Phat* record label. The rumor is that Caushun neither wrote, recorded nor rhymed live. He never put out an album. He was the face behind the farce! A public ruse! A fuckin' gimmick! That ain't homo-hop! Let me refer you to some real homo rappers!

We've heard of someone named "Misdemeanor" (Missy Elliot), but have you heard of someone named "FELONi?" There ain't a better straight woman rapper out here who she can't go rhyme for rhyme with! You can take words like "lesbian," "woman," and "feminist" from this rhyme-sayer's name and sit them in the corner! She is a true MC in the purest form. Her CD, *A Woman's Revenge* is one of the best rap CDs I've heard in years—a CD where every song is bangin'—no filler bullshit—and thank God, no special guest appearances from lesser popular rappers! Thirteen tracks of pure fire—all FELONi—A "Five Mic" classic CD! Definitely a homo-hop/rap classic. On her opening song **"No Fear,"** she comes right at you rapping, *"My mama never had a good man in life, for all you muthafuckas wantin' to know why I'm a dike!"* On her title track song **"A Woman's Revenge,"** a spoken word piece, she raps to the men, *"Try to change your world 'cause pretty soon no girl will be willing to bow down and suck your dick—especially after she—suck my clit … this is a New World Order and it involves some of your daughters."* Fuck what you heard (about gay and lesbian rappers)!

Debbie Harry (Blondie), Roxanne Shante, Salt-N-Pepa, Queen Latifah, MC Lyte, Monie Love, Sista Souljah, Yo-Yo, Lady of Rage, JJ Fad, Ms. Melodie, Lady Bug, Nonchalant, Lisa "Left-Eye" Lopez, Rah Digga, Charli Baltimore, Gangsta Boo, Da Brat, Queen Pen, Heather B., Mia X, Sole', Free, Foxy Brown, Lil Kim, Amil, Vita, Missy Elliot, Lauryn Hill, Eve, Trina, Gloria Velez, Khia, Remy Ma, Shawnna, Jean Grae, Jacki-O, Diamond & Princess (Crime Mob) and untested newbie phenom Lil Mama—FELONi is better than most of them and as good as any of them! Add her name to the pantheon of great female MCs. The rap game better not sleep on this chick FELONi! And she ain't the only lesbian rapper doin' the damn thang!

And this nicca Deadlee, the "gayngsta" rapper—another homo rapper who summons the spirit of Ice-T's CD *Body Count*. His CD, *Assault With A Deadlee Weapon*—a groundbreaking record, courageously contrived to dispel the myth of the soft, effeminate homosexual man. His rap style blends rap, rock, R&B and spoken word, woven together to fit his uber-hyper-masculine persona. And at the same time Deadlee exposes us to the woes of growing up gay in a masculine world with cuts like the soul-bearing **"Good Soldier II,"** which conjures up the ghost of Otis Redding with its heart-wrenching backup vocals. Again, fuck what you heard about gay rappers! Check the technique!

Anyone who does not want to see homo hop/rap succeed in the mainstream is the enemy of rap/hip-hop! Why? When you censor the growth of any artistic expression, you run the risk of killing it. Don't tell me what America isn't ready for! America wasn't ready for black folk to sit on the front of the bus either! And don't tell me that rap music's foundation is based on some superficial bullshit "street credibility!" You're a hypocrite and let me tell you why! When critics of rap criticize rappers for their lyrical content about guns, bitches, hoes, drugs and sex, rappers are quick to point out that movies show violence and killing all the time! And this is true! But the difference is that Stallone and Schwarzenegger don't carry their movie personas on their sleeves! Stallone is not Rambo in real life and every moviegoer knows this! Stallone and Schwarzenegger ain't ever been shot like Tupac and Fiddy! So the analogy between a Rambo (Fictitious) and a 50 Cent (certified gangster with a rap sheet) are bogus!

But so-called "gangsta rappers" claim they are what they rap about! They call it "Keepin' it real," "Keepin' it gutter." "keepin' it 'hood." And many of them have rap sheets to prove it. So the comparison is unfounded. We don't associate words like "killer," "thug" "gangster," or "menace to society" with Stallone, Schwarzenegger, Mel Gibson, Steven Seagal, Jet Li, Jackie Chan, Rock, Vin Diesel or any action hero movie persona when we see them in the street. Why? Because even the simplest among us know that they were just ACTING! You will never see Stallone at the Oscars mean-muggin' Mel Gibson and shouting, *"PPPP-Unit! ... Paramount Pictures Bitch!"* as he accepts his award. But when we saw Tupac, who was shot five times rap, *"Call the cops when you see Tupac! Pull your Glocks when you see Tupac ... we gon' kill all y'all niggas ..."*—when 50 Cent says he was shot nine times and raps, *"Front on me, I'll cut ya, gun butt ya ... I'll have yo' mama pickin' out yo' casket, bastard!"*—When Jay-Z raps, *"If you shoot my dog, I'm-a kill your cat ... I put my muthafuckin' faith in a Tech [9=gun]"*—when Rick Ross raps, *"Nigga try me, I'm-a teach his mama homicide!"*—When Trick Daddy says, *"I'm a thug!"*—When Young Jeezy and TI inform us about their trap star (selling drugs) days—when The Game raps about gang life, you better damn well know that they are what they rap about ... the so-called "street credibility" factor that you wouldn't question if you met them on the street! They don't stop being what they rap about and become nice citizens and wear suits and have aspirations to run for governor. Nay! They want you to believe that they will fuck you up in the street! And indeed, they will! Their thug persona is what helps sell their records. They've got 'hood rap beef videos. They walk the walk and talk the talk! When you read about them in rap magazines, their thug persona is clearly on display. Even the way they pose on the magazine covers. It's never a big cheesy smile with the words, *"I'm Rich Bitch!"* over their heads. Nah. They gotta mean-mug and ice-grill us as they floss their *Jacob* watches. Angry at nothin'! Got a million dollars and still can't find happiness!

A so-called rap expert appeared on the *Tyra Banks Show* and said that gay rap would never be acceptable in the mainstream rap world because rap is based on "street cred." Is he saying that a homo rapper does not have street credibility? And just what is street credibility? In its present incantation, "street cred" has to do with your reputation in the ghetto as a gang banger, drug dealer, thug, hustler, predicate felon, pimp, stick-up man, murderer, head bussa, battle rapper or a miscreant with a police record to validate you're persona. 50 Cent raps, *"I know niggas from your 'hood—You have no history!—Never poke nothin'!—Never pop nothin'—nigga stop frontin'!"* 50 Cent destroyed Ja Rule with verses like this, claiming that his street credibility was fabricated, thus nullifying Ja's gangsta and reputation in the 'hood. People like 50 Cent further create the illusion that a rapper must have validation from the streets. But that's not how rappers viewed each other in the advent of hip-hop. Street cred/gangsta rap is a sub-genre of rap!

Street cred was birth with the advent of gangsta rap. When rap first hit the airwaves, people weren't thinking, "Is this dude from the streets?" We were just happy to hear something new out of our community! We didn't question the street cred of Sugar Hill Gang, Grandmaster Flash and the Furious Five, Kurtis Blow, Fat Boys, Run DMC, Whodini, LL Cool J, Kool Moe Dee, Slick Rick, Doug E. Fresh, Big Daddy Kane, Beastie Boys, Eric B. & Rakim, BDP, Heavy D, Fresh Prince & DJ Jazzy Jeff, Salt-N-Pepa, Queen Latifah, Mc Lyte, Leaders of the New School, and even MC Hammer (who made street cred an issue by changing up his dance act for a thugged-out album called *The Funky Headhunter*, which exposed him as a fake gangster). Again, street cred came to the fore with the advent of gangsta rap acts like NWA, Tupac, Snoop Dogg, Ice Cube, Ice-T, DJ Quik, Biggie, Jay-Z, etc. The "street credibility" argument is the most bogus reason for keeping gays/lesbians out of mainstream hip-hop! If it were truly all about street cred, please explain how we got polka-dotted *Kwame*, suave *Special Ed*, super high-top fade *Kid & Play*, aesthetically challenged *Biz Markie*, backwards pants-wearing prepubescent *Kriss Kross*, college graduate *Young MC*, fake Jamaican accent rapping *Snow*, underwear modeling *Marky Mark and the Funky Bunch*, lip-syncing *C&C Music Factory*, Latin Adonis *Gerardo "Rrrrrrrico Suave,"* Snoop's certified rap son *Lil Bow Wow*, born into the rap game *Lil Romeo* and MC Hammer dancing impresario *Vanilla Ice*? Fuck <u>STREET CREDIBILITY</u>!!!!!!!!!! Bring back <u>STREET TALENT</u>!!!!!!!!!!

It's okay to call black women "bitches & hoes," but don't let those gay people tell their stories! It's okay for the 'hood man to rap about his days as a D-boy/snowman (drug dealer) and all of the criminality of "trapping," but those gay rappers gotta go? It's okay for rappers to tell us how they are fucking the be-Jesus out of our daughters, but don't let those fags rap about man love! It's okay to slide credit cards up black women's ass-cracks ala Nelly, but don't be rapping about a man suckin' another man's dick and liking it! It doesn't matter that Dr. Dre and Snoop Dogg had visions of homosexual sex with rapper Uncle Luke (Skyywalker) when they rapped, *"Gap teeth in your mouth, so my dick's got to fit ... Luke's bendin' over so Luke's gettin' fucked ..."* You can rap about homosexual sex if it's meant to degrade, dehumanize and emasculate a person—this is acceptable homoerotic poetry. It's acceptable that we bounce to the lyrics of the bling-bling materialistic nature of mainstream rappers who floss diamonds that our brothers in Africa dug up from the earth in an effort to support their starving families, but goddamnit, those fucking homos got no business in hip-hop! Damn we're some ignorant cusses!

Personally, I don't believe that rap music was ever intended to include gays and lesbians, just as it was not intended to include a parachute-pants wearing brotha from Oaktown (Hammer) or some silly white Jew-boys from the Bronx (Beastie Boys). But something wonderful happened—rap evolved! Those early South Bronx rappers didn't foresee a Beastie Boys, a Third Bass, a Vanilla Ice, a Bubba Sparxxx, a Paul Wall or an Eminem, who is arguably one of the best to ever spit on wax! This is the essence of Hip-hop! Hip-hop was founded with the same mentality that they claim America was founded—a melting pot of cultures, religions and ideas. The Statute of Liberty reads, *"Give me your tired, your weary, your huddled masses, yearning to breathe ... send these, the homeless, tempest-tossed to me ..."* That was the promise of America, but like America, hip-hop reneged and became the bastard love-child of mainstream America, frontin' like its all-inclusive when, in reality, hip-hop is a hypocritical child weaned from the breasts of its mother (America). America is male-centered and hip-hop is male-centered. Young brothas and sistas, huddled together in the ghettoes of America, yearning to breathe (have a voice) during the "tempest-tossed" era of Reaganomics and hip-hop was that way out. Hip-hop became the voice of the voiceless, decrying all of the social ills and hardships of living in urban America as a black heterosexual male (and to a lesser degree) and female.

And yet still, 30+ years in the rap game, no homosexual voice has been heard in the mainstream. Pathetic! Again, I say homo rap was never meant to be a part of hip-hop! Some of the earliest rap lyrics suggested that as such. In 1982, rapper Grandmaster Flash released, *The Message*, an ode to ghetto life. He hints at homophobia when he raps, *"Crazy lady/livin' in a bag/eating out of garbage piles/ used to be a fag hag ... Got sent up for a eight year bid ... spent the next two years as an undercover fag ... till one day you was found hung dead in a cell...."* He called homosexual/bisexual men "undercover fags." Today they are called "down-low" or "D/L".

Many of the new hip-hop fans of rap music don't know or understand where and how rap evolved. They don't know that rap was a movement among the ghetto-voiceless that grew out of the concrete jungle of South Bronx, New York. Rap and hip-hop represented change! It was no fad like Disco music! Hip-hop is to minorities, as Rock & Roll was to white folk—rebellion, liberation, and freedom to think outside the box. Rappers came on the scene and presented themselves in ways that were clearly in protest to what America stood for—baggie pants, oversized shirts, hats twisted backwards, tattoos, earrings, fancy cars, excessive/gaudy jewelry, profanity, creative vernacular (slang & Ebonics), etc. But along the way, the hip-hop community lost its way. Women became bitches & hoes, money became more important than the message, and talent was decided by which rapper could "diss" another rapper the best and payola. The truth be told, gay people were never even considered in the hip-hop equation for the voiceless, which is the hypocrisy of the hip-hop movement! Word!

I'm holding this book up before the hip-hop world and asking for a Reformation. Like Martin Luther (the 16th century German/Catholic monk), who nailed his famous *95 Theses* to the church door in Wittenberg, I'm nailing this tome on the door of hip-hop! And I'm looking to start a "Protest Movement"—not just against homophobia, but also misogyny, xenophobia, and the "minstrel show" that Wynton Marsalis so eloquently analogized. Let this book serve as the seminal work on the investigation of homophobia in hip-hop.

Meet the Homo-Hop Rappers ...

Cat Eyez

As the light shines on a new wave of hip-hop, where LGBT artists are in the immediate spotlight, twenty-two year old rapper **Cat Eyez** can be found and hard to be ignored. Dubbed hip-hop's **"Ghetto Prince Charming,"** **Cat Eyez** is out to prove that gay can also be gangsta. *"I've hung out in the blocks. I've seen people get shot! I've dated gangbangers and drug dealers. I had to go to the morgue to identify my first love's body! I know all about thug living. And yet, because I'm gay, I can't possibly be a hardcore rapper?"* He states, *"Gay people come from the 'hood too! Gay people buy rap CD's too! And gay people call a huge percentage of the game behind the scenes. So why can't we be center stage?"*

San Bernadino gay rapper Cat-Eyez

With his raw, in-your-face, stereotype-challenging lyrics, this multi-racial alley cat is out for his rightful place in the game. The fact that he's been through three failed record deals and had no album released, demonstrates his persistence and hunger to make it. He disciplined himself, perfecting his flow and learning to produce his own beats. He then set out to record *Cat-Astrophe,* his debut album independently. Soon, he came across **Milo Management** and became a regular guest performer in their showcases. His sexually suggestive single **"Kitty Box"** was one of the songs featured on their **Homo Revolution Tour CD.** Cat-Eyez has collaborated with artists like **Delacruz, Salvimex, Mélange LaVonne, Shorty, Roc, Bigg Nugg, Deadlee**, and **Foxjazell** just to name a few. He appeared in several protest shots in **Mélange LaVonne's** music video **"Gay Bash**." Representing the East and the West, sporting yellow tinted contact lenses, while performing in leopard print, this is one "cat" you've got to check out! **Cat-Eyez'** appearances are as ever changing as his song topics. And hopefully, he will continue to entertain and move us for years to come. **www.myspace.com/cateyez197.**

Veto Ali

Paid Dues recording artist **Veto Ali** is focused. I don't think you understand what focused means until you hear her talk about her album, *Chicago Hope.* *"This album is my heart, soul, my pride and joy. It's like my firstborn. I've done many albums before, but this is the first one I will be releasing to the public."*

Five years in the making, this album, from her grandmother's basement on Chicago's tough South-East Side, she recorded three LP's on only $800 worth of equipment. *"Me and my boy Reggie used to go in there and just rap our asses off! Every beat on my album and his [album] were all me. By 2002 Reggie had recorded **Street Structure** and then we drifted apart."*

Chicago lesbian rapper Veto Ali

During her four years at Luther High she met **Murda Ace**. *"Me and Ace immediately liked each other. We used to write shit and tell each other to read it. Always competition."* Soon **Veto** joined Ace's rap group, the now defunct **L.A.W. (Love Amongst Warriors)**. She and L.A.W. split thereafter and had an ongoing beef for two years and then called a truce. *"I didn't wanna see it go beyond rapping. It was sorta getting too personal. They talked about me and Reggie's facial features and we talked about their personal lives. I've got a daughter now, so I wasn't tryna be dead over some high school bullshit. I said, 'fuck it!' Let's just get money."*

By the time **Veto** graduated from Chicago's Luther High School South, barely passing with D's and enrolling at Columbia College Chicago (2003), she was armed with two solo LP's and a duo album with her friend Reggie a.k.a. **Frost**. *"My first album was called **Hace Mucos Anos**. My second album was **Le Morte De**

*Katalyst kuz I was calling myself **Katalyst** at the time. Then, me and Frost dropped* **Shut Up-Shut Down (The Game)***.*

Veto Ali grew up in a middle-class family, yet she chose to sell drugs from the time she was nine until she was seventeen. *"I think the guys feel me because I go through the same things that they go through as well—the baby mama drama, the issues with having to feed your child, messing with the women—all of that!"*

Veto Ali's fierce flow and unapologetic style are of mythic proportions in Chicago's South Side. Her rhymes are filled with pain and anger over a child who grew up fatherless, but watched her dad take care of other girlfriends' children. *"It's all on the album—the mixtapes. I don't hide how I feel about my father. I don't like his ass! I love him but I don't like him. I could never respect a man who does that to his family."*

The hype surrounding **Veto Ali's** new album *Chicago Hope* is astounding considering she hasn't dropped a mixtape to let herself be known citywide. *"'**Kiss The Girls'** is like my introduction. I'm reppin' for all of the butch lesbians out there who wanna say these things but can't rap, ya dig? I do it for them. I do it for the entire Rainbow Community because nobody is reppin' for us out there hard enough. I'm not sayin' I'm gonna wear rainbows all over my clothes, but I let it be known what I stand for and what I'm in to."*

In 2006 **Veto Ali** and long time nemesis **Murda Ace** teamed up and formed the crew, **South Side Paper Brigade**—hence the name of the label **Paid Dues**. *"I'm not tryna change the game. I just wanna let folks know females can rap and I'm one that do it damn good! I want people to listen."*

Despite the love from her fans, today, **Veto Ali** feels empty inside. On May 9, 2007, her biggest fan/supporter and only sibling Roy, died from heart failure. *I didn't wanna rap anymore. I didn't have anyone to cheer me on, so I felt like 'fuck it!' But everyone kept telling me, 'Roy wouldn't want you to stop rapping. He would want you to keep it up ... so I'm doing my second mixtape and dedicating it to him."*

With the lost of her brother Roy deeply etched in her soul, **Veto Ali** is setting the streets of Chicago afire this summer with her single **"Hey Girl,"** which has already played on **Power 92.3**. Expect to hear big things about this South Side girl with boyish good looks.

www.myspace.com/vetoali85

Pam Jones

A Star is born! 2007 is the year of female rap/hip-hop artist **Pam Jones.** Born in Cincinnati, OH. This sista is lighting up the west coast! There have been female rappers from New York and from the South, but there's something missing from the West. **Pam Jones** calls Cali (Los Angeles) her new home—home of palm trees and sunny weather; she's redefining the sound of female MC'ing with her in-your-face brand of rapping.

Los Angeles transsexual rapper Pam Jones

Growing up listening to the sounds of The Notorious B.I.G., **Pam Jones** knew her destiny was to bring the game West Coast style—becoming hot in Tupac's stomping grounds. Not since 1992 when Yo Yo was tearing it up has there been a female rapper who's ready to grab the reins of rap and ride it until the wheels fall off! It is truly a new day! This chic **Pam Jones** is known everywhere—from Cali to Atlanta, they call her **Pam Jones International.** The top bitch is here! Unsigned at the moment, but looking to start a bidding war among record execs. **Mediatakeout.com** named her the **"The New Rap Star."** Her debut album *No More Misses Nice Bitch* is set to be released in 01.01.08. Check for it!

www.myspace.com/thequeenofthewestcoast

<u>Bigg Nugg</u>

Based out of Ohio and representing the gay "Bear" community, **Bigg Nugg** mixes it up with his thumping beats and spitfire lyrics on all types of things, ranging from personal struggles to equal rights. A musician since his teenage years, the metamorphosis and transition into the artist known as **Bigg Nugg** was a natural evolution of talent. His lyrics are filled with reflection, passion, and a yearning for the balance of power in a homophobic society.

Ohio gay rapper Bigg Nugg
Photo credit: Donato Sepulveda

Bigg Nugg's first full-length album, titled ***La Revolucion*** was released in the spring of 2007. The album has tracks produced by **Homegrown Music, N1, Tori Fixx,** and **Bigg Nugg**. Special guests on the album are **JFP, soce—the elemental wizard, Delacruz, Deadlee, Q-Boy,** and **Tori Fixx.**

Bigg Nugg has been featured in various blogs—from **AfterElton.com** to **Gay365.com**. His music has received airplay on stations from Pittsburgh to Houston and was featured in **Bear Tracks Compilation CD** before his first full length CD was released.

Bigg Nugg was one of the artists that played all ten dates of the historic **HomoRevolution Tour**—the first ever, regional tour of gay, lesbian, Bisexual,

Transgendered music artists. After **Bigg Nugg's** Los Angeles performance, **Tiina Teal** of **L.A. Records** commented, *"Ohio native Bigg Nugg, one of our personal faves personified a very KRS-One old-school vibe with his positive, physical energy."*

Clearly, **Bigg Nugg** is a rising star in a burgeoning genre, offering his own unique style, in a way that will transcend cultural boundaries.

www.myspace.com/biggnugg

White Lesbian Rapper

White Lesbian Rapper a.k.a. **WLR** (real name: Alicia Leafgreen) started rapping at the tender age of ten. Originally inspired by the works of **Vanilla Ice**. Since then, she has gone on to do live shows all over the United States. She describes her style of rap as "Old School-New Style Hip-Hop." This artist is inspired by the works of Old School Hip-Hop music and is working to revive that old school style, through modern-day hip-hop. Described as a "rap artist who is lesbian," instead of a "lesbian rapper." The name **"White Lesbian Rapper"** comes from an all out honest approach to rap. *"I just want people to know who I am up front and not be fooled by lies or betrayed once they buy my CD. I'm an honest person and that's what my music is about. I pride myself on appealing to all people in my rap, not just the homosexual community."*

Minneapolis lesbian rapper White Lesbian Rapper "W.L.R."

www.myspace.com/Whitelesbianrapper

El-Don

A gangsta rapper whose lyrics are so subtle regarding his homosexuality that only the perceptible ear will hear a hint of homo-thugness in his message. **El-Don** grew up on the mean streets Newark, New Jersey. At age 10 he began rapping. *"I was kinda shy as a kid and rapping brought me out of my shell. It also helped me break the ice with the straight boys that lived around my way. Growing up, I was raised around girls, so I learned a lot of their ways and mannerisms. (lol) Dudes around my way thought I was soft until I started rappin' in freestyle battles—against some of the best at that time. It felt good to be a gay male and shuttin' a straight dude down in a freestyle battle!"*

New Jersey gay rapper El-Don

These freestyle battles won **El-Don** respect in his 'hood. It is not easy getting respect in the 'hood as a gay man, but this is one emcee who took his! **El-Don** says, *"In the straight world of hip-hop you have to prove yourself—and if you're gonna be gay … you gonna have to really come with it to be taken seriously and that's what I did!"*

El-Don wrote his own raps and freestyled with straight cats. The shit that he rapped about was raw, real and nothing soft. He did not want to come off as what straight people perceived a gay man to be. In his rhymes, there is no distinc-

tion between his manhood and his sexuality. Perhaps the most hardcore gangsta gay lyricist out here, **El-Don** takes no prisoners when it comes to his rhyme schemes. **El-Don** says, *"Basically, I feel if we gay peeps are gonna really hit the mainstream in hip-hop, we really gone have to bring it and be ready for all types of beefs and battles because they will surely come."*
www.myspace.com/elhiphop

<u>Mz. Fontaine</u>

British lesbian singer/rapper **Mz. Fontaine** is a cut above the rest. She possesses the talent, drive and determination to maintain her status as a proclaimed star. With the ability to cover Soul, British Neo Soul, Hip Hop and R&B, she is a versatile and dynamic individual who prides herself on achieving her goals. This caramel-toned, smooth-talking gentlewoman with a suave demeanor has been known to attract the eyes of many straight women. With the majority of her fan base residing outside of the UK, her soft-spoken voice glides over the waters to embrace the audience, further adding to her sex appeal.

U.K./England lesbian rapper Mz. Fontaine
Photo credit: Tim Aldcroft & Greg Frederick

Originally, a native Guyanese (South American), **Mz Fontaine** had shown interest in the entertainment sector from the start. Coming from a musical background, she first performed at the tender age of five (accompanied by her mother) at the very prestigious "Cultural Centre" in the city of Georgetown.

Mz. Fontaine shone in the spotlight. Her confidence grew rapidly so that by the age of twelve, she had a collection of performances under her belt. She was certain of her future career but was taunted and confused about her sexuality in her early teens.

Reaching the age of seventeen, she made the bold and confident step to be a proud lesbian. "*I'm very open and have been since I found myself and became happy and comfortable in my own skin as a young black and proud lesbian."*—**Rainbow Network** Feb. 2006

In 2002, she was crowned **Miss Butch** at the **UK's National Lesbian Beauty Contest**, where she utilized the platform to perform the very controversial **"Pass Dat Crutch."** There, she made her mark as the UK's **First Out** lesbian singer/ rapper.

This led to demands for performances at a vast array of leading LGBT events and with that added burst of confidence, **Mz Fontaine** focused on promoting her musical talent and style with appearances across the UK, Europe and the USA. *"There aren't many lesbian rappers like me, but more are starting up. They approach me after shows and say I've inspired them. That's nice."* **Marie Claire Magazine** 2005

Autumn 2005 saw the delivery of her highly anticipated album **"New Era."** Inspired by the revelation of her LGBT community, **New Era** was not just a method expressing her own sexuality, but a symbol of gender identification and sexual orientation. *"Being different is a learning process. And that's the message Mz Fontaine, Pride London's latest and only black Patron hopes to get across loud and clear."*—**EuroPride Magazine**, UK July 2006

Spring 2007 sees the upcoming release of **Mz Fontaine's** first single **"Tick Tock"** off the forthcoming album *Spoken Thoughts.* To promote its release, **"Tick Tock"** was featured on **Showtime's** cable television series *The L Word* (season four) along with plans to film the coinciding music video to aid its promotion.

Developed behind the poetic aspect of spoken words, the album *Spoken Thoughts* is a musical expression into the world of Love, Pain and Politics. It is a sound compilation of personal thoughts that will easily be incorporated into the life of the everyday listener and LGBT community alike.

"Mz Fontaine is one of the stars of a new wave of rap and hip-hop ... With a critically acclaimed album under her belt, performances at high profile gay community events and collaborations with artists in the UK and the US, Mz Fontaine is one to watch."—**RainbowNetwork.com,** UK February 2006.

Mz Fontaine just finished touring in America with the **Homorevolution Tour** where she headlined with other homo hip-hop artists.
www.myspace.com/mzfontaine www.mzfontaine.com

Diamon D.I.V.A.
a.k.a.
<u>The Gay Queen of Hip-Hop/Florida's GayDaughter.</u>

Will Homo-hop ever go to the next level? Trina, Trick Daddy, Jacki-O, Rick Ross, Pitbull, and of course, Uncle Luke are some of the big names that put South Florida on the map.

Hailing from the 305, the mighty M-I-YAYO, the Dirty-Dirty Dade County, introducing Miami's own **Diamon D.I.V.A.**, *Florida's Gay Daughter, the Gay Queen of Hip-Hop*! Born Kenyatta Bryant, **Diamon D.I.V.A.** grew up on the mean streets of Miami's inner-city Liberty City. At the age of ten, he was introduced to Calvin Mills, producer and manager of the teenage group *The Puppies*, which he performed with for five years.

Miami gay rapper Diamon D.I.V.A.

Diamon D.I.V.A. grew up and finished high school. He went on to pursue his education in Kentucky where he received degrees in Culinary Arts and Computer Technology & Business. In between studies, he missed performing. Writing music in his spare time to ease the sensation of not performing, music was never far from his heart and passion. There came a day when **Diamon** lost a very special friend, which sent him into depression and caused him not to write any music for over a year. After months of depression over the loss of his best friend, **Diamon** sat down and began writing what would become his first single, *"Life Ain't Easy" (Time Moves On),* an ode to his dead friend. With the support of family and friends **Diamon D.I.V.A.** wrote 19 more tracks for his CD *Designated Era*. Thus, the beginning of **Diamon D.I.V.A.'s** CD's *Caution* (1998), *Homo Thug* (2000), and *Exclusive* (2002).

After recording four CD's **Diamon D.I.V.A.** decided to take a break. Something lacked in his musical life. *"One day I was invited to a huge straight party, but I didn't have anything to wear, so I went to the flea market and picked me up a pink T-shirt. I got the Pink Panther airbrushed on it with the quote, 'Taste Da Rainbow Bitch'. At the party, everyone noticed my pink Tee.... A boy with a pink Tee? This was when that song 'White Tee' was out. My homegirl who invited me was one of the D-Jays. She gave me the mic and I started rhyming 'MY PINK TEE' and the crowd went up!*

That led to **Diamon D.I.V.A.'s** recording hit singles *"My Pink Tee," "That Nikka,"* and *"Whoa My Pussey, Pussey,"* which played on Internet Radio, Miami radio 97.7, 89.5, 93.5, Da Doo Dirty Broadcast Show, Gay Hip-hop show and landed him a variety of interviews. He went on to write gay anthems like *"We All The Same,"* and *"Why U Lookin' At Me?/I'm A Fagget,"* which received national attention. **Diamon D.I.V.A.'s** goal is to further open the doors of hip-hop and let homo-hop get its just due and he won't stop 'til 'cause it's hip-hop!

www.myspace.com/FLAGAYDAUGHTER

Delacruz

Originally from Watts, California, **Delacruz,** a proud mother who knows all the struggles of being a single parent, lesbian, female and a woman of color. She has a lifetime of experiences and she has only just begun to get her stories out.

Cali lesbian rapper Delacruz

Delacruz is an out and proud Lesbian MC who is holding absolutely nothing back! A self-proclaimed stud, she raps about everything, from so-called "lesbian" women who sleep with women—and men and lie to women about it, gay pride, gay bashing, her feelings on Bush (and the President too), equality and more!

Delacruz is a seasoned stage performer. In 2004, she performed at the **Long Beach Pride Festival.** She has numerous club appearances under her belt. In March 2007 **Delacruz** embarked on the **HOMOREVOLUTION TOUR** with other LGBT artists, performing over ten cities in four Southwestern states. The coming year will take **Delacruz** to the next level.
www.myspace.com/delacruzmiller

(Bone) Intell

Intell (aka Bone). Ya favorite rapper's favorite gay rapper. A "gay rapper"—not a rapper who "raps gay." The newest, hottest MC to ever be called "homo" and a rapper who has burst onto the scene to push the Homo-Hop Movement forward for 2007 and beyond. Originally, hailing from Buffalo, NY, Intell has been rapping since he was twelve. Growing up on the mean streets of New York, to say that Intell had a hard life is an understatement! Gang banging and run-ins with the law were the norm. Out on his own at seventeen, gang life became Intell's haven and provided him with his life experiences. Realizing and accepting that he was gay in an environment that would not accept him, Intell saw that his life wasn't where he wanted it to be. At nineteen, Intell decided to make a turn for the better and dedicate himself to his number one grind—his music. Now based out of Long Island, NY. Intell is gearing up to set the Homo-Hip-Hop movement ablaze!

Long Island gay rapper (Bone) Intell (right)
and the homies throwin' 'em up.

Intell's music is for people who understand the struggles of growing up on the streets and having to fend for self. It is for those who have faced adversity for being who they were born to be—whether gay or straight and have come out on top. Intell is here to bring clarity to those gay men who are out in the world that live every day the way they have to in order to survive. Intell wants his fans to know that he is HOOD and he is GAY, but above all, he is a man and to respect him as a man. Real talk!

www.myspace.com/boneintell

JenRO

*"On stage, **JenRO** looks like your average aspiring hip-hop star with mic in hand, hat cocked to the side, baggy jeans and a hip-hop attitude that is both cool and confident. A quick scratch below the surface reveals ... that **JenRO** is anything but average. **JenRO**, from the Bay Area is one of the smartest and most creative hip-hop artists to emerge in recent years. Far from a gimmick, **JenRO** has the skills and beats to blow away the typical stale male rappers. With lyrics about sexual identity, self-acceptance and hanging out with her homegirls, **JenRO** might be one of the most honest MCs rapping today."*

—**Gay & Lesbian Times,** Portland, OR.

JenRO is a recognizable figure in her South San Francisco neighborhood: navy blue bandana folded over her forehead, tattoo of the Golden Gate Bridge scrawled across her right forearm, pants baggy enough to hide her slight 5'3" frame. She answers her cell phone with the sharpness and urgency of a numbers runner, spitting her habitual greeting three times in a row, *"What's the deal, what's the deal, what's the deal?"*

San Francisco lesbian rapper JenRO

Typical "San Francisco-reared gangstress" might be your first impression of **JenRO**, until you see the random collection of objects scattered around her bedroom: A furry zebra-striped bedspread, a Pride calendar with dates scribbled in permanent marker, a desk cluttered with cologne, amps, lava lamps, empty Pueblo Viejo bottles, CDs from Jen's favorite artists in rap, merengue and reggaeton. Most noticeable of all are the baby-blue walls covered with images of the standard-bearers of West Coast gangsta rap: **Equipto, Snoop Dogg, Playa Rae, Tupac, San Quinn, Messy Marv, Killa Tay** and—larger than all of them—her name spray painted in black graffiti letters.

It's not usual for a 21-year old newbie MC to situate herself in a pantheon of big names. What's striking about **JenRO** is her inclination to mix the different sides of her personality, making the seemingly disparate words she inhabits—queer, Latina, gangsta—all of a piece of her. On her Album, *Hate It Or Love It,* she spits lyrics about everything—from street hustles to hooking up with fly girls. Watching her take the stage in settings as far removed from each other as **San Francisco Pride** to **San Quentin Prison**—where **JenRO** has performed with the nonprofit anti-gang organization **United Playaz**—you wonder how easy it is for a queer female artist to embrace the contradictions of her sexuality and her gangsta consciousness and express them in a genre, whose penchant for misogynistic and homophobic lyrics seems like a prohibition against women in general, and queer women, in particular. But **JenRO** enjoys pushing the limits of the medium and she looks at the labels others might use to describe her with a blend of ambivalence and disregard. Ultimately, she insists, *"I choose to say who I really am!"* And if her honesty means she can't front like a mack daddy, she's not worried—she's got plenty more to say.

www.jenro.net
www.myspace.com/jenro

Salvimex

Juan Pacheco a.k.a. **Drastiko** created the rap group **Salvimex** in 2002. **Salvimex** members are **Drastiko** and **Cruz,** two hot bisexual Latinos. **Salvimex** means the union of two cultures—El Salvador and Mexico. **Salvimex** represents its own musical movement ("The Urban Movement") of the Latino communities of Los Angeles. They write their own songs in Spanglish slang. Their first CD, *Uniendo Fuerzas* was released in December2005.

Los Angeles Bi-sexual rappers Salvimex

Salvimex made its first group presentation in Oakland, California at the **PEACE OUT HIP HOP FESTIVAL** in 2004. That same year they also performed in Los Angeles (Echo Park), California at the **Latin Pride Festival,** which featured **Drastiko, Tercer Discipulo** and Cruz.

In 2005 **Salvimex** made its comeback at the **San Francisco Pride Main Stage**. Since then, they've performed in numerous venues, such as Plaza Mexico of Lynwood, Ca., Plaza Olvera in downtown Los Angeles and **Cinco de Mayo** festival in Anaheim, Ca., on local Los Angeles channels 22, 63 and channel 62 on the **"Los Angeles en Vivo Show"** and of course, many nightclubs in the Los Angeles area.

www.myspace.com/salvimex
www.bombasticrecords.com
www.myspace.com/milomanagement
Booking info. 323-422-5169.

FELONi

FELONi is a radical hip-hop recording artist born and raised in Detroit, MI. She also spent some of her elementary years growing up in Dothan, Alabama. At age 16, **FELONi** began writing and rapping in her bedroom. She would write prose and poetry in an attempt to release the internal anger she housed for many years since childhood. **FELONi's** mother was always on the run as a victim of domestic violence. As a result, **FELONi** often changed schools and neighborhoods. Poetry and prose became **FELONi's** refuge.

Detroit lesbian rapper FELONi
Album Cover credit: David Anderson

In 1993 several years after the violent murder of **FELONi's** brother and the attempted murder against her mother by her ex-boyfriend, **FELONi's** life took a drastic turn. Two of her poems, **"Caskethouse"** and **"Psychological Details"** were published in two local colleges' student newspapers. She also began to read publicly in local poetry cafes in Detroit. Inspired by the response and the sense of spiritual growth, **FELONi** continued to explore creative writing in poetry and hip-hop.

In 1998 **FELONi** began to focus more on releasing an album. She says she knew it would be difficult to get a record deal being herself and she did not want to change who she is just to get a deal. *"Fame was never important to me. In fact, I'm a very private person,"* says **FELONi**. *"However, it is important to me that my music be heard, because it focuses on a reality that many people don't want to talk about."* **FELONi** continues. *"I know the odds are against me, but I'd rather be hated for being who I am than to be loved for being somebody I'm not."*

FELONi's sound and subject matter is like no other mainstream female hip-hop artist out there right now! **FELONi** mixed and recorded over 85% of her controversial debut album *A Woman's Revenge*. She also wrote the album and is the Executive Producer. **FELONi's** debut album was self-released on her independent label, **Trak Diamond Records** in February 2007 (Black History Month).

One of **FELONi's** goals in music is to push the limits of hip-hop's sexuality by flipping the script on male posturing in an attempt to open up discourse on issues of human rights, sexual orientation discrimination, domestic violence and misogyny. **FELONi's** debut album has a strong "rap" overtone, layered in "hip-hop" consciousness. With irony, skill and catchy beats, **FELONi** uses the controversial complexities of hip-hop's language to challenge the burgeoning ignorance and hypocrisy within the world and hip-hop culture. **FELONi** states that many "rap" artists are not only selling their souls for fame and fortune, but they are selling their mother's soul as well.

FELONi's music transcends race, gender and sexual orientation because she speaks on an undeniable truth. **FELONi's** most "controversial" song "Brand New" took the hip-hop community by storm with the stinging hook, **"I Took Your Bitch!"** This song alone, garnered an incredible amount of attention and controversy across the world within both heterosexual and LGBT community. Since the release of *A Woman's Revenge*, **FELONi** has inspired countless others to tell their story of being gay or lesbian in a predominately homophobic society. To date, **FELONi** is the most known "out" urban hip-hop recording artist in the country based on "word-of-mouth" alone.

www.myspace.com/FELONi www.TRAKDIAMONDRECORDS.COM

soce, (pronounced so-SAY), the elemental wizard

soce, the elemental wizard is the Jewish, Gay, White MC. A computer programmer on Wall Street by day ... Level 27 Hip-Hop Spellcaster by night! He has been described as the male Lil Kim and the Jewish Eminem. soce's been on **MTV, VH1, Logo, HERE**, the **Source, URB, Out Magazine** and numerous German, Austrian and Swiss magazines, as well as being interviewed live on **WNYC 93.9 FM** and **Sirius Satellite Radio**, on OutQ 106, Raw Dog Comedy 104, and **Shade 45**. The **wizard** has been filmed in three documentaries on gay rappers.

New York gay rapper soce, the elemental wizard

In addition, he's produced tracks and performed as a special guest—rapping, singing and playing violin for numerous talented artists, including **MF Grimm, Jeff Lewis, dub-L, Mistermaker, Q-Boy, Bigg Nugg, Danny Katz, Sair, Many v.e.r.s.e.s., Kontrast, Chris Fuller, Frank Grimaldi, Jenn Lindsey, Linda Draper, Johnny Dangerous** and **Jon Berger. soce** produced the track **"Lick It"** by **God-Des** and **She**, which has become one of their big hits and they recently performed it live on the finale of *The L Word.*

Soce does live shows throughout NYC in not only hipster bars and clubs, but also at high schools, colleges, theaters, museums, community centers and synagogues. He's also done shows in Berlin, London, Sheffield (UK), Boston, LI, CT, NH, NJ, SF and has upcoming shows in Chicago, Iowa, Minneapolis, Mountain View, San Diego, and Los Angeles. He also programs his own flash cartoon videos and games.

When you're ready for a wild and exciting stage show, hit up **soce, the elemental wizard** for the latest beats, CDs, t-shirts, music videos and anything else you can dream of. If you've ever had to struggle, been in love, enjoyed a good role-playing game or just wanted to experience rap music where you can actually relate to every word spoken, **soce's** music is for you. **soce** has released three CD's—***Dream de la Dream*** (2003), I'm ***In My Own World*** (2004), ***The Lemonade Incident*** (2005). So come on, what are you waiting for? Check out **soce** at **Greathiphop.com** today.

www.myspace.com/soce **www.socetew.com**

Foxxjazell

"I don't aim to be the best or greatest rapper. I aim to be the voice of my people 'cause our voice is non-existent in the hip-hop community"—**Foxxjazell.**

Rapper **Foxxjazell** is a 5'10" striking mocha beauty that happens to be **transgender**. However, don't let this little "biological/physiological" gender assignment have you thinking that she can't flow with the best of them! She has performed for thousands of people at the world famous **Arena** nightclub in Hollywood. She also opened for 90's divas **Robin S., RuPaul.** And **CeCe Peniston**.

Cali transgender rapper Foxxjazell

Foxxjazell Keva Jackson was born in Birmingham, Alabama to a family of hardworking hustlers. Both her mother and father worked all types of odd jobs to keep food on the table. At age six, she became influenced by the likes of **Salt N Pepa, Michael Jackson** and **Madonna**. *"I would lock myself in my room and pretend I was performing in front of millions of screaming fans."* As she grew older, her parents didn't share the same vision that she did. Instead, they encouraged her to pursue a career more "logical" like teaching or nursing.

By age seventeen, **Foxxjazell** had graduated from high school with honors and was looking to conquer life as an entertainer. Her musical influences had advanced to **Tupac, Da Brat, TLC** and **Biggie Smalls.**

Leaving the South for stardom, **Foxxjazell** bought herself a one-way ticket to Hollywood with less than $20.00 in her purse. While in Hollywood, she started off modeling with a few print ads and also booked music video gigs doing background work. She quickly became discouraged when she realized these gigs didn't take her to the next level. A change had to be made.

The change came in the form of 14 year-old Maurice Tito Lopez, a runaway kid with big dreams of superstardom. The two young artists quickly teamed up and began making and performing music together. They eventually formed a group named **One20five** with two other local rappers. **One 20five** performed at various venues throughout Los Angeles, but eventually disbanded in late 2004.

Since then, **Foxxjazell** has performed throughout California, reaching new fans and expanding her fan base. She performed at **Latin Pride2004, PBE Music Festival, RU Talented TV Show**, and **San Diego Pride2003**. She did a benefit show in Las Vegas in August 2005 for **Hurricane Katrina** victims. **Foxxjazell** also performed in San Francisco in December 2005 for a benefit show for **Toys For Tots**. In 2006 she performed at L.A.'s **Club Flame** and the **Texas Summer Music Conference**. In March 2007 **Foxxjazell** stepped up her visibility when she appeared alongside rappers **Deadlee** and **Tori Fixx** on **The Tyra Banks Show**, garnering national attention. She also took part in the historical **HOMOREVOLUTION TOUR07**, which featured gay, lesbian, bisexual and transgender rappers. The future is bright for this unique young lady.
www.myspace.com/foxxjazellmusic

Shorty Roc

Brooklyn has had its share of groundbreaking entertainers. First there was **Big Daddy Kane** and **MC Lyte**. Then there was **The Notorious BIG** and **Lil Kim**. Next to put his mark down is the infamous **Shorty Roc**.

Brooklyn gay rapper Short Roc

Shorty Roc burst on the scene in 2003 with his underground smash **"Ten Gay Commandments,"** his rendition of the classic **DJ Premiere** produced **Biggie** joint **"Ten Crack Commandments."** He took his music to the streets with this banger and performed at clubs such as *Langston's, The Legendary Warehouse, The Clubhouse,* and *Sunday Nights at The Lab,* gaining underground praise for his street delivery, catchy punch lines and his heavy performance along the way. He had put out at an initial mix tape called, *"The Mixtape: Jackin' Beats,"*—hot flows on top of some of the hottest hits, which made its way through the NY gay hip-hop circuit. Topics ranged from the troubles of dating, society and the growing rate of HIV and AIDS.

Shorty Roc has participated in numerous festivals, including the famous **"Peace Out East,"** an annual music arts festival of lesbian, gay, bisexual, transgender and queer hip-hop artists, activists, fans and supporters in New York City. Other festival appearances include the **2007 Brooklyn Pride**, the **"Peace Out**

South" in Atlanta, **2006 Philadelphia Black Pride,** and **Memphis Black Pride** to name a few. Other notable performances include a showcase at the legendary **"Nuyorican Poets Café,"** **POCC 2006** family day in Commodore Park and a listening party sponsored by **GMAD** (Gay Men of African Descent). **Shorty Roc** is also being featured in a documentary titled **"Homophobia in Hip Hop,"** which is currently being screened at college campuses across the country.

2007 has been a landmark year for **Shorty Roc** with a memorable performance at New York City's Bryant Park as part of a **NYC Pride event, Splash nightclub, Brooklyn Pride, FacesNY Pride** float, his participation in the historical **HomoRevolution Tour** and numerous press articles including, **The Clik Magazine, NEXT Magazine, Bleu magazine** and **Uneq** magazine, a full page photo in the nationwide publication **THE ADVOCATE.**

Shorty Roc has just released *Personal*—his first full length CD of original material. It is available on both CD Baby and ITunes. The CD contains the controversial track **"Rappers Delight"** in which he ponders whether big-name rappers "get down." *(Objects of speculation and adoration in this case include 50 Cent, Snoop, Ja Rule, and Ludacris).* He plans to promote *Personal* through performances, festivals, professional appearances and the Midwest dates that are a part of the Fall swing of the **HomoRevolution Tour.**

Shorty Roc believes his purpose is to talk to the Community about issues in their lifestyle such as, safe sex, dating, troubles with society, and pride for self. His long term goal is to cross over as a hip hop artist—regardless of sexual orientation.

www.myspace.com/shortyrocdamic

Ricoshade (pronounced Ric.o.chet)

Main Entry: 1 Female (pronunciation fe.male) 1. of, relating to, or being the sex that bears young or produces eggs: having some quality (as gentleness) associated with the female sex.

Main Entry: 1 Emcee (pronunciation em.Se) Function: noun: Master of Ceremonies.

Ric.o.chet: (pronunciation ri.ka.shay) Etymology: French. Function: noun. A glancing rebound (as of a projectile off a flat surface); also: an object that ricochets.

A perfect tale of rhyme meets girls. A love story starring **RICOSHADE** … Longevity in the hip-hop world is a rare but coveted crown. There is but a handful of performers that have sustained long-term careers in the face of all the upheavals that rappers have to contend with in this era. Now do the math and multiply that times two and you will recognize the plight of a woman in the dog-eat-cat world of hip-hop. As a lesbian woman, who's trying to gain leverage in the hip-hop game, you have to double your efforts to knock down stereotypes, while breaking barriers while producing cutting-edge rhymes that are vital to both the streets and hip-hop's all-encompassing commercial machine.

Cali lesbian rapper Ricoshade

Enter Cali born and raised **Ricoshade**, a.k.a. a **"Female Emcee."** Once thought to be an instantaneous underdog in the bout, she is rising to meet those challenges and countering with a few punches of her own! **Ricoshade** grew up listening to some of hip-hop's most influential artists and groups like **Salt-N-Pepa, KRS-1** and **Tupac. Ricoshade** knew early on that she too had something to say and hip-hop would be that very same vehicle in which she would drive home that voice.

Upon realizing her dreams, **Ricoshade** set out to accomplish her goals of becoming a force to be reckoned with in the hip-hop community. Not a stranger to hard work, her talents have been exhibited and developed by performing at local talent shows and countless non-profit organization events.

Determined to make her mark an impressionable one, **Ricoshade** has twice paid her dues by hitting the **Black College Tour Circuit** and opening for high caliber artists like **Mystikal, Ludacris,** and **Ice Cube** to name a few. She further added to her credits by performing for local access cable shows and appearing on the national television shows **"Showtime At The Apollo"** and **MTV's** *The Cut w/Lisa "Left-Eye" Lopez* as well as repeat special invitations to appear on the memorable *Keenan Ivory Wayans Show.*

Seasoned in the game with over 10 years dedication to honing her skills, **Ricoshade** is out of the trenches and ready for combat. She has mastered her art and has an arsenal of talent to prove it. She effortlessly combines meticulous wordplay with a signature wit and style that is a diversified reflection of her poignant five genre talents.

Concurrently, **Ricoshade** has been perfecting her stage show to hold true to her hard earned reputation of captivating audiences with her undeniably explosive verses and venomous delivery. With her eclectic blend of versatility, staying power, drive, energy and skill, she gives a glimpse as to what the future holds for hip-hop. We'll be there as she charters this voyage across old and discovered terrain. So get those umbrellas ready! There's a storm coming!

Ricoshade Entertainment
www.ricoshade.com
www.myspace.com/ricoshade1

Deadlee

DEADLEE has garnered much press with his groundbreaking, genre-screwing approach, attracting cover stories in **Gay City News** and **Choice** magazines and feature stories in the **Long Beach Press Telegram**, **Las Vegas Review Journal**, **Las Vegas Citybeat**, **Dallas Voice**, **Albuquerque Alibi**, **San Antonio Current**, **Frontiers** and **Dot News Magazine**. His involvement in the first ever regional tour of GLBT hip-hop artists sparked mentions in the press from the **New York Daily News**, **Rolling Stone**, **Wired Magazine**, **XXL Magazine**, **The Advocate**, **L.A. Weekly**, **Philadelphia Gay News**, **Urb**, **Instinct** and **Variety** to name a few. **DEADLEE** was interviewed, not once, but twice, by **CNN**—once for the **Paula Zahn Now Show** on homophobia and hip-hop and the second time for **CNN Entertainment** for the launch of the **HOMOREVOLUTION TOUR 2007.** He appeared with fellow LGBT hip-hop artists Tori Fixx and Foxxjazell on the Emmy-nominated **Tyra Banks Show** on April 13, 2007 and on June 7, 2007 **DEADLEE** appeared on The Howard Stern Show (Sirius Radio) where he and Howard exchanged jokes and pleasantries. Mr. Stern gave his support to **DEADLEE** and homo-hop.

Los Angeles gay rapper Deadlee
Photo Credit: Marla Rutherford

DEADLEE launched his career earlier this millennium. Initially, his style was a blend of hip-hop and rap, with a thrash rock undercurrent. His lyrics tackled race, class, sex, and even police brutality. **DEADLEE** earned a position as a key player in music's latest underground movement—gay rap/hip-hop. He went on to play a variety of music festivals, including the **Peace Out Festival** (Homohop) in Oakland, **Peace Out East** in NYC, **HomoAGoGo** in Olympia, Washington, **Los Angeles Latin Gay Pride Festival**, **Christopher Street West/Los Angeles Pride Festival** in West Hollywood, the **San Francisco GLBT Pride** Main Stage two years in a row and **Outfests' FUSION Festival**.

Said **Gay.com's** Josh Tager, *"Like many of his rap peers, Deadlee's albums are intense, writhing outbursts of anger. The notable distinction here is that when Deadlee bashes, he's bashing back. He is a vigilante for social justice, committed to confronting homophobia wherever he sees it."*

DEADLEE has provided music for a variety of motion pictures, including *On The Downlow* and *Vengeance*. He was also one of the eighteen gay hip-hop artists featured in the landmark documentary film on gays in hip-hop called *Pick Up The Mic*, which was picked up by the *LOGO* network, after making the festival circuit. **DEADLEE** was also in a **LOGO** reality show called **"Hip Hop Homos"** and the video for his **"Good Soldier II"** song played both on the channel's music shows (New Now Next and The Click List). He has two CD's, *7 Deadlee Sins* and *Assault With A Deadlee Weapon* under his belt.

DEADLEE has made inroads with his acting and is a member of the Screen Actors Guild (SAG). He has performed in several movies, including *Vengeance* and *Dead Men Walking.*

DEADLEE also dabbles in stand-up comedy and has appeared before stunned laughing audiences at the **Ha Ha Caf** ... and various stand-up comedy venues throughout Los Angeles.

Late 2007 will see the release of **DEADLEE's** third CD, entitled *Intifada,* which will feature collaborations with Phoenix's DownLow, the UK's Qboy and the Pet Shop Boys! Working with old and new producers, *Intifada* will feature the tightest beats and a few hook-laden hits, while also featuring a few tracks that mainstream the classic **DEADLEE** sound that his fans over the past seven years have come to know and love. *Intifada* will be the CD that will expose **DEADLEE** to a new generation of listeners who had no idea he existed.

www.myspace.com/deadleeofficial www.deadlee.com

(Shout out to these other gay & lesbian rappers—Pretty Boy, God-Des & She, DaLyrical, Katastrophe, Mélange Lavonne, Miss Money, Shante Smalls, M.C. Flow, Unecc, Katey Red, Sugur Shane, Jonny Cash, Sgt. Sass, Smut Stud, Scarletto, Rigo-

mortis, Hissy Fitt, Sonny Lewis, Kiyle, Fat Rat, Nicky Click, Aggracyst, Scream Club, The Phenom, Grand Royal, Phat Family, Maasen, Cazwell, Houston Bernard, Dyamond Theory, Julie Fuckin' Potter "JFP", Best In Da Game "B.I.G.", DJ Johnny Turok, Dutchboy & DJ Monkey "Rainbow Flava," Morplay, Money The B-Girl Wonder, Operator Burstup, Double-K.I., Nfamus Tha Kid, Tru Bloo, TruDog, Lisp, Captain Magik, Hanifah Walidah, Dion-Punk of the South, Cashville Vicious, Sissy Nobby, Anye Juha, Karter Louis, Elite, Illicit life Ent's. Triple Threat and DJ Jeffa). Homo-hop is comin'!

To all of these gay, lesbian, bi, transgendered rappers and MC's I say keep doing what you are doing! You are iconoclasts—icons—and when the history of this rap game is documented, you shall be mentioned amongst the torch-bearers of this new and exciting genre of hip-hop, homo-hop. This book stands as a testament that homo-hop has arrived and each one of you has arrived and all of you reppin' homo-hop are revolutionaries, unlike the masses, who follow what's popular and chic and mainstream. You are hip-hop! Let the haters do what they do—hate! Let the homophobic Internet thugs and naysayers do what they do—hate! These Internet fiends have no life! Their comments are just the vain babbling of uninformed hate mongers. They are brave behind the screen of a computer, full of bravado and nastiness. They have no life and will never amount to anything other than what they were created to do—HATE! Fight the good fight and be strong and courageous. Khalil Amani.

On Those Preachers &
Their lies ...

"His watchmen [preachers] are [spiritually] blind: they are all igno-rant, they are all dumb dogs, they cannot bark [warn us of things to come]; sleeping [with everybody!], lying down, loving to slumber. Yea, they are greedy dogs which can never have enough [sex, money, fancy cars, power, praise & chicken dinners], and they are shepherds [pastors] that cannot understand [the errors of ages gone by]: they all look to their own way [teaching], every one for his gain [what he can get from his members], from his quarter [church]" (Isaiah 56:10-11).

Pretty much every mainstream preacher or televangelist on TV has had their say about homosexuality. Yes! They say homosexuality is against God's Law. Because there's a law in the Bible prohibiting a man from sleeping with a man (and by the way, there is no law in the Old Testament about a woman sleeping with a woman), this they call "proof" of God's divine law.

I will concede—if we take the Bible for its literal truth and believe and adhere to every scripture within its pages, then one will come across a condemnation of homosexuality. In Leviticus 20:13 it positively states, *"If a man also lie with mankind as he lieth with a woman, both of them have committed an abomination: they shall surely be put to death"*. In that same book it further states, *"Thou shall not lie with mankind as with womankind: It is abomination."*(22:18) And then comes the story of Sodom and Gomorrah in Genesis 19, which appears to be anti-homosexual. In the New Testament Paul's writings in Romans 1 and Jude carry the homophobia over to Christianity. Yes! Absolutely! The Bible condemns homosexuality! But the Bible also condemns the eating of pork! But the Bible's Judeo-

95

Christian interpretation is DISHONEST in its dissin' of gay people! The historical reasons for these laws being written are never taught in the church.

These preachers pick and choose which "truth" they should espouse. Like homosexuality, the Bible also condemns eating pork, catfish, shrimp and lobster (Leviticus 11). How many preachers love to eat a Thanksgiving Day or Christmas ham? How many preachers love a plate of spaghetti and catfish? The Bible makes it clear that fish without fins and scales are not eatable—like catfish and shrimp. The Bible tells us to steer clear of swine (pork), yet most of us eat bacon, pork chops and *Honeybaked* hams.

These preachers will tell us that it's okay to eat that which God forbade in the Old Testament and quote one scripture (from the New Testament) to "prove" that God changed His/Her mind. But God said, *"I change not ... "* (Malachi 3:6). So who do we believe—God or the lying preacher? Why is it that preachers harp on the law concerning homosexuality but say nothing about the eating of swine? How and why do they pick and choose what is "God's Law" and what scriptures are to be thrown in the garbage can?

The Christian preacher who's been to seminary school has been brainwashed with some wonderful justifications for keeping part of God's Law and destroying the other. They teach that Christ's coming did away with the Old Testament Law. They say that we don't live under the "law" anymore. We live under "grace." Yet, whenever they want to make a case against homosexuality they find themselves reading Leviticus of the Old Testament. They go from the book of Romans 1 straight back in time! Homosexuality was a part of the OLD TESTAMENT LAW! So again, is it "Law" or "Grace" Christian preachers?

This is the hypocrisy of Christianity—using certain passages to bolster your faith and omitting other passages that you don't like and then concocting bogus precepts, dogmas, creeds and catechisms to support your "gutter" religion—not the true teachings of Jesus, but the bastardization of his message!

Let's examine Jesus for a minute. Jesus was a Jew! (Matthew 1, Luke 3, Revelation 22:16, etc.) No preacher will contest this fact! As a Jew, Jesus would not have eaten pork! As a Jew, would he have gone into a church or a synagogue? The answer? *"As his custom was, he went into the synagogue on the Sabbath day and stood up for to read"* (Luke 4:16). Jesus' custom was to go into a SYNAGOGUE (a Jewish church) to hear the Word of God. Non-debatable! Now here's another question. What is the Sabbath day? The Answer? The seventh day or Saturday. So why do Christians go to worship (church) on the first day (Sunday) of the week? Here again, the preacher has wonderful reasons why the change from Saturday to Sunday, but the historical reasons are clearly known through the Catholic

Church, the Mother Church of the World. Jesus did not change Saturday Sabbath worship! The Catholic Church did! And then here comes her bastard children, the Protestant Movement who followed the Catholic Church's decree. So, in essence, if you're a Baptist, Methodist, Episcopalian, C.O.G.I.C., C.O.G., A.M.E. etc, you are kissing the ass of the Roman Catholic Church and dissing Jesus' custom of seventh day (Saturday) worship!

Christians say they believe and follow the Ten Commandments (Exodus 20:3-17). They are LIARS! The fourth commandment says, *keep the Sabbath.* Christianity violates the seventh day Sabbath of the Ten Commandments only to turn around and lean on the homosexual prohibition! Homosexuality is not a part of the Ten Commandments! The Ten Commandments are supposed to be the moral compass on which the rest of the Laws of God revolve around yet, the Christian preacher, knowing full well what the Bible says about the "real" Sabbath goes along like a child hiding behind his mother's skirt and follows the paganistic practice of Roman Catholicism. Phucking spineless!!!

But oh when it comes to homosexuality ... Protestant Christianity becomes a roaring lion, seeking homosexuals to devour! If your Christian god can change His Sabbath from the seventh day to the first day, might it possible that He changed His mind concerning homosexuality? If he reneged on his dietary laws concerning the eating of unclean fish and pork, could there be an inkling of a chance that the law concerning homosexuality was for a purpose and a time and has become of non-effect?

The popular "orthodox" view is that Jesus never spoke on homosexuality. The mentioning of Sodom and Gomorrah is as close as Jesus comes to dealing with homosexuality (and even then he was using these cities to illustrate inhospitality). In Matthew 5:22 Jesus says,

> *"But I say unto you, That whosoever is angry with his brother without cause shall be in danger of the judgment: and whosoever shall say to his brother, 'Raca', shall be in danger of the council: but whosoever shall say, 'Thou fool' shall be in danger of hell fire."*

What does it mean when Jesus says, *"whosoever shall say to his brother, 'Raca' shall be in danger of the council?"* What does "RACA" mean? This is the only time in the entire Bible that this word is used! "RACA?" *Hmmmm?* Some scholars have suggested that "raca" was the equivalent of calling a man a FAGGOT! What? "Raca," in its popular definition is defined as "worthless," "empty-headed," "vain," "good-for-nothing," "to spit." But check it! The word "Raca" is derived from the Hebrew word "Rakh," meaning "soft," "weak," and "effeminate" and is used today as a euphemism for GAY MEN. Could Jesus have been commenting on homophobia—warning people not to call people names like "faggot" back in the day? "… *whosoever shall say to his brother 'Raca' shall be in danger of the COUNCIL.*" The "council" today is the freethinkers in our society who would call out the homophobe for his bigotry. The "council" is a body of people who can think critically about a subject and make recommendations and reprimands—like when a homophobic athlete says he hates gays—penalty for your bigotry? Loss of endorsements, publicly humiliated, and made to recant his ignorant remarks and apologize to those offended. Jesus could've easily said, "*Anger shall get you judged, homophobia (name-calling) will get you embarrassed, and calling someone a fool will get you a one-way ticket to hell!*"

The scholar, Joseph Wallfield (aka Warren Johansson) made the "raca" connection and postulates that Jesus, indeed, spoke out about calling people out of their name—using homophobic language. This does not, in no wise, suggest that Jesus was pro-homosexual, but shows his compassion for people who were deemed "different" or in the minority. Jesus was liberal, tolerant and didn't view homosexuality as some great hell-fire sin! Jesus was a man, who no doubt was influenced by cultural conditioning and quite aware of the sexism, racism and homophobia of his day, just as he was keenly aware of the Roman exploitation of his countrymen. Jesus was a man of his times who was ahead of his time.

Today, they ask the question, "*What would Jesus do?*"(WWJD) Would Jesus have been critical of homosexuality as many of these preachers are today? From all of the biblical evidence, it is highly unlikely that you would have heard Jesus in an angry homophobic diatribe on a sunny Shabbat afternoon like we hear from our preachers during Sunday service. The historical Jesus ran with those who were considered outsiders, lowlifes and the scum of society. The Bible refers to them as winebibbers, publicans and dogs. These lyin'-ass preachers today wouldn't be caught dead hanging out with a gang banger or a prostitute. They are too busy bragging about the Rolls Royces they own, while their parishioners drive Chevrolets—"Cheve" one foot and "lay" the other and walk your ass to church! You got poor people in your church and you're living the high life! Ostentatious! Profligate! Downright greedy for mammon (greed/worldly gain)! Motherfuck a "Pastor's Day!" He can wait until he gets to heaven and be rewarded like the rest of us! Why should the people waste their hard earned money on a goddamned Rolls Royce? Just 'cause a nigga can preach and looks good in a three-quarter pinstripe suit? A Cadillac used to suffice as the pimpmobile of choice for many preachers, but these new-jack preachers ain't fuckin' around when it comes to stuntin'! I guess they're singing Lil Wayne's song, *"Stuntin' like my daddy!"* Our Father God is a stunna, so we are stunnas!

These jackleg preachers—these hallelujah hucksters—these pulpit pranksters are the most homophobic in our society—using God as a weapon, they rant about the evils of homosexuality. They all parrot the same lie about homosexuality. Listen to them! *"I'm against homosexual marriage and I'm against the homosexual lifestyle because the average life expectancy of a homosexual and lesbian in the United States is 42 and 45, versus 75 and 79. These people are fighting for a lifestyle that is robbing them of half of their life expectancy,"* says pastor Rod Parsley. *"I don't think its God's best ... I never feel like homosexuality is God's best,"* a sheepish pastor Joel Osteen says. *"All homosexuals will be burned alive!"* Benny Hinn roars. *"You cannot say I was born this way! I don't care what scientists say! Homosexuality and lesbianism are spiritual abortions,"* so says a more scientifically enlightened bishop Eddie Long. *"Homosexuality is Satan's diabolical attack upon the family. AIDS is not just God's punishment for homosexuality; it is God's punishment for the society that tolerates homosexuality,"* rants a confused Jerry Falwell. *"Hollywood Jews are promoting lesbianism, homosexuality and other filth,"* says a self-righteous Minister Louis Farrakhan.

This is the prevalent thinking among religious folks. And they all use the Bible to justify their stance on homosexuality, but you're just about to get the raw truth on how they came to believe the negative trash on homosexuality. You are about to find out what none of them have ever taught! I'm about to expose you to the 3,000 year old polemic (argument) that has been sheepishly challenged—a goddamned religious lie that has been perpetrated as THE TRUTH—dressed up in a holy robe, forged with God's signature! Oh these fucking preachers! They say homosexuals can change their lifestyle and become straight, yet they can't seem to stop getting their dicks sucked by prostitutes on a sunny Sunday afternoon ("I have sinned" Jimmy Swaggart). They claim to speak for God, but they've got their dirty hands in the cookie jar, stealing money (Rev. Jim Bakker). They condemn fags to hell, yet buy $900,000 houses for their Christian whore mistress, while pocketing another $8,250,000 (that's eight million plus) to maintain their immoral lifestyle (Rev. Henry Lyons). They rage against homosexuality, but secretly got a "downlow" fetish for male masseurs and crystal methamphetamines (Ted Haggard). They claim to have the anointing of God on them, while they're giving their wife the "hard-bottom special," (stomping her on the ground) treating her like a whore that held back her pimp's money (Bishop Thomas Weeks III)! They boast about their blessings from God—their Rolls Royces, mansions, and jewelry, while their parishioners give all that they can in hopes of receiving similar blessings (Rev. Ike, Bishop E. Bernard Jordan, Rev. Fred K.C. Price, Rev. Creflo Dollar, Rev. T.D. Jakes, etc.). They are all multimillionaires! *W.W.J.D.?* He damned sure wouldn't flaunt his wealth to his followers!

Enough ranting! Now, the real deal!

Homosexuality:
The Great Sin of Sodom?

✦

(Deconstructing the Biblical Myth
Against Homosexuality)

○ ○

"The sin of Sodom was not that men were punkin' one another up the ass!
Their 'sins' were inhospitality, lying, thievery, adultery, fornication, rape, idolatry, and murder. These people were homosexual, bisexual and HETEROSEXUAL!"

—The Author-

"The idea that the fundamental sin of Sodom was homosexual behavior is not present in the Old Testament."

—The Eerdmans Bible Dictionary-

Now we come to the final chapter! This is the historical breakdown of how homosexuality became a so-called "sin" against God. I saved it for last because I want your undivided attention. This whole book rests on this chapter. When you finish reading this chapter you will be forever changed in your thinking about homosexuality. You will NEVER hear this information in church for several reasons. The first reason is that most preachers are BOUND by the Christian faith and cannot deviate from orthodoxy. Any teaching that appears to deviate from the Christian message is deemed heretic. The most notable mainstream preacher who broke the ranks of traditional Christian teachings was Rev. Carlton Pearson. For his actions he was made a religious pariah (outcast) among the brethren.

Another reason you will not learn this information in church or Sunday school is because many so-called men of God don't know it! And if the preacher doesn't know this stuff, then surely the laity (commoners) is in the dark.

For the author, finding out the reason for the anti-homosexual law in the Bible was just like when I found out there was no Santa Claus. I was pissed that I'd been lied to! I was livid that it took me THIRTY-SIX YEARS to discover the historical truth for the Bible's condemnation of homosexuality. I, like most Christians had been brainwashed to accept anything my Baptist preacher had to say on the subject. It didn't help either after I converted and became a Hebrew Israelite—the lie continued—and the same scriptures and story were used to justify the murder of homosexuals—the Sodom & Gomorrah myth. And even having minored in religion in college, the truth about homosexuality remained elusive.

No man taught me what you are about to read—not my Christian upbringing, my Hebrew Israelite conversion, nor my college religion courses. This truth came from above! All of the Christian sermons by your favorite televangelist can't undo what really happened way back when to cause the Bible writers to concoct a myth, which was to be the moral pretext for human sexuality. Yes! I'm calling any preacher who condemns homosexuality as sin a goddamned, bold-faced lying dog! Now let's get to this TRUTH!

(*This essay is reprinted and revised from Khalil Amani's book, ***Ghetto Religiosity II: Uncovering The Naked Truth,*** 2001.)

I've decided to write this essay in response to the growing controversy over legalizing gay and lesbian unions/marriages. I am particularly disturbed by the Christian answer to this debate. Although there are a very, very few churches that respect the rights of gays and lesbians, the vast majority of Christendom is against their unions. Let me state my position right up front before I systematically and historically deconstruct the very hypocritical Judeo-Christian-biblical argument against homosexuality.

First, I am 100% pure black heterosexual masculine-man, but I believe that gays and lesbians should have the right to marry and live as fruitful lives as any heterosexual. I believe that the government should stay the hell out of consenting adults' bedrooms! As a black man, conscious of the prejudice, bigotry, hatred, racism, classism, and sexism that has been perpetuated on black people in the name of "religion" and "Christianity" by white so-called Christians, I can be nothing but sympathetic to their cause. Some have made the argument that you cannot equate sexual preference with discrimination of minority groups. I say BULLSHYT! The same paradigms and systems and people are doing the discriminating ... white people, and white males in particular—that's where the power to effect change emanates. And really, it doesn't matter to me if there is no comparison between sexual preference and racism. WRONG is WRONG and it is WRONG as hell to hate or deny others the right to live productive lives because you don't like their choice of mate!

Blacks and Hispanics don't have the power in government to effect any real change in Washington! Just look at the makeup of the Senate, Congress, House of Representatives and the Judicial branches of our government—mostly (old) white men.

We did not come into this world "knowing" that homosexuality was wrong! Where did we get it? What books and scholars shaped our minds to be of this opinion? Not one scholar and not one book, save the Bible, brought us to our present thoughts concerning homosexuality.

These Right-Wing, pseudo-conservative, Republican, Bible-toten racist white people want things to return to the old ways. They came out against gays and lesbians like gangbusters! Led by such ass-holes as the Rev. Jerry Falwell (R.I.P.) and his "Moron Majority." Did I say "MORON?" I meant Moral Majority. Falwell attacked AIDS as the "Gay Plague." He said, *"A man reaps what he sows. If he sows seed in the field of his lower nature, he will reap from it a harvest of corruption"* (Jones 226). If that's true Falwell, what will America have to pay for her crimes against the Native American and the African? Remember that little event in our country's history, euphemistically called, "That Peculiar Institution?" SLAVERY and the annihilation of the indigenous population, the so-called Indians! Shall America *"reap what it has sown?"* Shall *"he that leadeth into captivity go into captivity*, Falwell?" Shall *"he that killeth with a sword be killed by the sword*, Falwell?" How shall America answer before the JUDGMENT SEAT (Daniel 7:9) for exterminating the Native/Indigenous people of the Western Hemisphere? Huh? Shall the *"sins of the (your white fore) fathers be visited upon you"* racists and homophobic crackers today Falwell? Answer me goddamnit! You want to quote Bible, so let's do it!

If the homosexual has hell waiting on him/her, how much more does an evil country that has murdered untold millions and millions of its people have coming, Mr. Falwell? You think a little "ass-fuckin'" and a little "pussy-lickin'" is worse than what has happened in this country's wretched, shameful, and deplorable history? I beg to differ! You, Falwell, are a hypocritical, self-righteous, beam-in-your-eye bastard! The Bible says, *"And why beholdest thou the mote [speck] that is in thy brother's eye, but considerest not the beam [rock] that is in thine own eye? ... thou hypocrite"* (Matthew 7:3-5).

America condemns the homosexual and relegates him/her to the hellfire, but considers not what she as a country has done. So, if you want to "search the scriptures" to lead homosexuals to hell, I'd suggest that you put that at the bottom of your list because there's going to be many more heterosexuals in hell than there will be homosexuals.

Ex-Presidential hopeful, Patrick Buchanan announced that homosexuals had *"declared war on nature, and now nature is extracting an awful retribution"* (Jones 226). It wasn't until AIDS started affecting middle-class, churchgoing housewives that the Reagan Administration started dealing with it seriously. What these suckas like Falwell and Buchanan need to do is stop blaming homosexuals for AIDS and call for a Congressional Hearing on the work being done at Fort Detrick, Maryland! They might find AIDS' origin and cure there! Can you say the words, "TUSKEGEE SYPHILIS EXPERIMENT" boys and girls?

The Bible can be used to justify any, and I do mean any position a person has. It was used to justify slavery, ethnic purity, and the subjugation of women. Now, it is being used by Christians to direct gays and lesbians to hell. If Christianity is truly against homosexuality, all factions need to make it part of their doctrine. But this is not the case. There are openly gay congregations, preachers, priests, and lay-members that find themselves within the Body of Christ. Are they in denial about their ultimate damnation for being homosexual?

In Judaism and Islam, the law is clear on the homosexuality question. It is an offense against their god. But these Christians! They are some double-minded, lukewarm, wishy-washy, straddling-the-fence, and middle-of-the-road folk who can't "officially" decide if their religion and god condemns or condones homosexual behavior. Now I'm going to lay it to rest for anyone who has an ear.

My first question to destroy the biblical argument against homosexuality is this: "What is the Christian doctrine on salvation? Are we saved by works of the law or are we saved by faith through the grace of Jesus Christ?" (Ephesians 2:8-9) This question is fundamental to this debate. The answer is FAITH and GRACE. This is how we are saved. Christian preachers say stuff like, *"This is the second dispensation." "Grace is the way 'cause the law took a fall!"* I'm not saying that Jesus taught this. I'm saying this became the "orthodox" view of the Christian faith. Remember … grace, not law! The law was done away with in favor of Gentile grace as taught by Paul.

So, why is it that many preachers and anti-gay and lesbian folk revert back to the Old Testament Law (which, by-the-way, was not written for a Gentile audience) to make a bullshyt point about the condemnation of homosexuality? We've heard preachers say shyt like, *"Women shouldn't preach!" "Men shouldn't wear ear-*

rings!" Read Exodus 32:2-3 and see that earrings were a unisex item! Our wives, daughters, and sons wore them fool! It was a cultural thang just as it is today for men to wear earrings in both ears. Some folks teach that earrings had something to do with slavery and branding but the truth-of-the-matter is that earrings are an African and biblical cultural thing that can be traced back thousands of years. So let's tell the whole truth!

Holiness preachers teach that women shouldn't wear pants because the Bible says, *"A woman shouldn't wear that which pertaineth to a man"* (Deuteronomy 22:5). Again, this is Old Testament Law given to the Jews ONLY! Besides that, the writer/s weren't talking about pants when it was written circa 444 B.C.E. No one wore pants back then! They all wore some unisex shyt called ROBES, TUNICS, and CAFTANS … men, women, and children! Wasn't no damned pants back then! So why would a preacher in the 21st century come along and interpret Deuteronomy 22:5 as a prohibition against women wearing pants? I'll tell you why! 'Cause a stupid ass-wipe like that doesn't know a damn thang about EXEGETICS (critical explanation or analysis, interpretation) or plain ol' biblical history! In his ignorance, he tries to interpret some 3,000year old shyt in the context of today's American religious jargon. He doesn't know that, *"that which pertaineth to a man"* had to do with TRANSVESTITISM … women wearing wooden dildos (dicks, penises as part of the Goddess religious practice! See **The Interpreter's Dictionary of the Bible**, Crim et al., p. 818, Supplementary Volume). Another so-called Law from God to keep Israel from practicing other folk's religion. Go research it! Those silly-nilly "Je-hopeless Witnesses" teach, "Abstain from blood" (Acts 15:30). But didn't Jesus say, *"Whosoever eateth my flesh, and drinketh my BLOOD, hath eternal life … For my flesh is meat indeed and my BLOOD is drink indeed"* (John 6:54-55)? But I know what you're saying, *"Oh, that's just figurative language!"* Tru' dat! Meanwhile, these folks have corrupted the meaning of "abstain from blood" (to fit their pseudo theology) and caused some to die from a much needed and easily performed blood transfusion! But the ROOTS of "abstain from blood" and "women forbidden to wear that which pertaineth to a man" are the Old Testament Law! These pseudo-Christian laws ARE NOT some new shyt that Jesus invented! No! No! They are inventions out of the mind of that myth-maker Paul and later Christian Church Fathers that are based on Old Testament Levitical Law. They are based on Mosaic Law!

Most churches believe that it is a sin to dance, smoke, drink, go to a nightclub, or have sex before you're married. None of these things are supported by concrete biblical scripture! All of these "laws" that Christian preachers try to impose on their congregations are rooted in Old Testament Laws that doesn't even pertain to them. Out of one side of their mouth they say, "The Law is dead!" Out of the other side of their mouth they say, "God's Law is against homosexuality!" What is it? Law or Grace? If homosexuality is against God's Law, why not eating pork and shrimp or practicing the Sabbath on Sunday? Why do they pick-and-choose?

Scholars have come up with what they call the "Noahide" or "Noachian Laws." These are laws that were supposedly given to Noah after the flood (in Genesis 9, although they are not mentioned) that all people, including the Gentiles, were to follow. The Noahide laws are written in the Babylonian Jewish Talmud (Sanhedrin 56a;cf Pseudo-Phocylides), which cites seven more laws that are binding to all people.

> They [the Gentiles] were to recognize government, avoid blasphemy and idolatry, refrain from bloodshed, resist robbery, and abstain from eating flesh cut from a living animal, and refrain from adultery (Myers et al., p.766).

Homosexuality is not part of the Babylonian Noahide laws. Adultery is! But Not homosexuality! Sex is on the menu, but it is a prohibition against adulterous sex … heterosexual or homosexual.

Sodom and Gomorrah

Now let's get to the crux of biblical condemnation of homosexuality. All that we believe about homosexuality is rooted in the Old Testament story of the destruction of two cities—Sodom and Gomorrah. You can read the story in Genesis 19. Whenever a preacher wants to show how God hates these so-called "faggots" and "dikes," he pulls Genesis 19 out of his ass! The story has been taken out of its historical context! Let's investigate the "Sodom and Gomorrah God hates homosexuals" story and see what a sham and a lie we've been taught. Genesis 19 says:

> And there came two angels to Sodom at even; and Lot sat at the gate of Sodom: and Lot seeing them rose up to meet them: … And he said … my lords, turn in … into your servant's [my] house, and tarry [wait] all night … And they [the angels] said, Nay [no!]; but we will abide [stay] in the street all night…. And he [Lot] pressed [begged] them greatly and they [angels] … entered his house…. But before they lay down, the men of the city, even the men of Sodom, compassed [surrounded] the house … both old and young, all the people from every quarter: And they called Lot, and said unto him, Where are the men which came in to thee this night? Bring them out to us, that we may know [fuck] them [up the ass]. And Lot went out at the door … and shut the door … and said, I pray [beg] you, brethren, do not so wickedly

[don't try and rape these men], I have two daughters which have not known [fucked a] man; let me, I pray you, bring them out unto you, and do ye to them as is good in your eyes: only unto these men [angels] do nothing … (19:1-8).

First of all, this is another clear example of sexism in the Bible. Lot was willing to let the men of the city rape his two virgin daughters to save these two "angels." How cold and phucked-up can a father be? Secondly, this story proves that the men of Sodom were not exclusively homosexual, else Lot would have never offered up his two daughters as a sacrifice to indulge in their wickedness. If these men where exclusively homosexual, why would Lot offer his two daughters? That's like trying to feed meat to a vegetarian! Clearly, they were Hetero, Homo, and Bi men and women tryin' to rape these angels. Yes, there were even women involved in this mass orgy-to-be. That is clear from the verse "all the people from every quarter." Thirdly, if Lot understood that he was in the presence of angels (and it is clear that he did by the deep respect and hospitality shown them), he should have known that they had the power to deal with the situation before them and not blab out to the men to take his daughters.

And so Christians have taken this story and taught that it was exclusively a Homo/fag thang goin' on. Sodom, was supposedly exclusively inhabited by "Sodomites" (homosexuals) and their wickedness was so great that God killed them for being gay. That's the party-line teaching in the Christian church. Sodom was the "San Francisco" of its day. Full of faggotry! So why were Lot, his wife, children, and sons-in-law (and I would assume, their families) living there? This proves that Sodom WAS NOT an exclusively homosexual city, as we believe. It proves that Sodom was just like San Francisco is today (or any major city in America for that matter with a gay community). Again, Christians, through their ignorant preachers have been misled about the reasons for Sodom's destruction. **The Eerdmans Bible Dictionary** writes this on the subject:

> Sodom, often with Gomorrah, became proverbial for conspicuous sinfulness that is ripe for judgment … and destruction by God … The IDEA THAT THE FUNDAMENTAL SIN OF SODOM WAS HOMOSEXUAL BEHAVIOR IS NOT FOUND IN THE OLD TESTAMENT and appears ONLY in later documents of the New Testament (Jude 7, II Peter 2:6-10). The Hebrew and Greek words translated "sodomite(s)" at Deut. 23:17, I Kings 14;24; 15:12; 22;46, II Kings 23:7 and I Timothy 1:10 concern homosexual behavior (male cultic prostitution in the Old Testament pas-

sages) BUT DO NOT INCLUDE IN THEM ANY ALLUSION TO SODOM AS DOES THE TRANSLATION (Myers et al., p. 959).

Ouch! You might want to read that again ... very slowly! What this is saying is that the Hebrew Old Testament word for Sodomite (Qades) has to do with a religious practice (so-called male cultic prostitution) and not homosexuality in-and-of-itself. Again, **The Eerdmans Bible Dictionary** says, *"THE IDEA THAT THE FUNDAMENTAL SIN OF SODOM WAS HOMOSEXUAL BEHAVIOR IS NOT FOUND IN THE OLD TESTAMENT AND APPEARS ONLY IN LATER DOCUMENTS OF THE NEW TESTAMENT."* You got it? This whole idea of Sodom being destroyed by God for being faggots didn't originate in the Old Testament and is not part of Jewish folklore! It is a New Testament creation and invention. It is Christian lies and interpolation! The ancient Jews who heard and read this story did not view it as an act of God against homosexuals. Those allusions are New Testament inventions.

This should be a revelation! In a few, I'm going to explain to you the real reasons for Sodom's destruction. For now, it is enough to know that Sodom's wickedness was not that men were fucking men! Its crime was pure lawlessness and disregard for life. They were liars, thieves, fornicators, adulterers, idolaters, rapists, murderers, and all around law-breakers! These people were homosexual, bisexual, and heterosexual! Genesis 19:4 says, *"the men of the city, even the men of Sodom ... [and] ALL THE PEOPLE FROM EVERY QUARTER."* See it? "All the people!" Clearly, everybody, male and female, gay and straight, took part in this maddening scene. It was pure "mob mentality." Their sexual preference is not what led to their destruction.

The reason the "homosexual motif" stands out is because the scriptures let us know that it was a homosexual faction that led the assault on the two angels. They were the leaders. "All the people" followed their lead. We saw these men trying to phuck these angels and we got tunnel vision! Yes we did! Sex always catches our eye. But now, if you go back and read Genesis 18 where Abraham, the father of the Jewish nation, the man from which Judaism, Christianity, and Islam sprang, pleads and begs and tries to get God to see his side of the story and not destroy Sodom! Abraham tries to debate God on the grounds that He will be killing the innocent with the wicked. Abraham, six times, tries to talk God out of destroying Sodom.... six times! If Sodom were a city of homosexuals, why would Abraham try to defend them? He didn't just plead his nephew Lot's cause, but the whole city! Sodom was not just some faggot town! Sodom was a thriving city with its own problems of lawlessness. No different than any major city today.

Again, for the third time, with major redundancy!, *"The idea that the fundamental sin of Sodom was homosexual behavior is not present in the Old Testament."*

So where did we get our ideas about Sodom and Gomorrah's destruction from? Let me tell you! From your preacher and his New Testament historically fraudulent books, Jude and II Peter. These books make the issue of Sodom's wickedness homosexuality. In Jude 7 it states, *"Even as Sodom and Gomorrah ... giving themselves over to fornication and going after strange flesh [same sex unions], are set forth for an example, suffering the vengeance of eternal fire."* See how Jude honed in on the homosexual act? God and Abraham (in the Old Testament) never stated Sodom's specific sin. They just said they were unrighteous and great sinners. If! ... If homosexuality was one of the sins of Sodom, it was far from the only sin or the main reason for the city's destruction! Jude does not want us to know that there were many more heterosexuals that were burned up with the Sodomites/homosexuals. Jude wants us to believe it was strictly a faggot-thang! But what do we really know about the book of Jude? Nothing! Well let me tell ya! Jude was written ca. 100-130 C.E./A.D. That's about 1,700 years after Sodom's destruction and about 100 years after Jesus' and Paul's deaths. The two biggest proponents of Christianity (Jesus and Paul) didn't use Jude as a source because they were already dead when it was written. We don't know who the author of Jude was, for surely it wasn't Jude. Its literary style suggests second-century authorship. The philosopher Voltaire said in reference to Jude's quoting the Book of Enoch:

> Jude, in his epistle, quotes Enoch more than once; he uses his very words; he [Jude] is so devoid of good sense as to assure us that Enoch ... has written these prophecies. Here then are two gross deceptions, that of the Christian who invents the Epistle of Jude ... there was never a CRUDER LIE (Applegate 153).

Boy! That Voltaire doesn't bite his tongue for shyt! He calls the Epistle of Jude a "crude lie!" From his viewpoint, what does that say about Jude's understanding of the Sodom story? ... It's straight-up whack! Professor Burton L. Mack, a John Wesley scholar of the New Testament, says this of the book of Jude:

> The tenor [tone of Jude] is morose and the mythology extremely gross [filled with a lot of garbage, e.g. angels, heavenly hosts, the devil, fallen angels, scoffers, and fire] ... And nothing is gained by the confusion of authorial voices [several unknown authors]. Jude is simply a matter of sloppy literary production (210-11).

Damn! And that's from a Christian scholar! Knowing this, you can no longer rely on Jude as a "credible," "valid," and "reliable" source to diss homosexuals. Knowing how phucked-up the book of Jude really is, your understanding of Sodom's destruction must be reworked.

The other reference to Sodom as a gay town comes from II Peter 2:6-10 which apes Jude.

> And turning the cities of Sodom and Gomorrah into ashes condemned them ... [Blah, blah, blah....]

Now what do we know about this book, II Peter? Again, the answer is nil ... nothing! I'm starting to feel like *Fire Marshall Bill,* "LET ME SHOW YA SOMETHIN'!" II Peter was written ca. 150 C.E./A.D. or 120 years after Jesus' death. Do you know how much stuff changed from Jesus' day until 150 C.E.? Lots! It was a time of great Christian myth-making and II Peter and Jude were part of that myth-making. Professor Mack further writes:

> The message of 2 Peter is not much different from that of Jude, the letter that was used as a source.... The so-called Petrine tradition [Peter's works] was created in the second century [100-200 C.E.] by means of pseudony-mous [false name] writings attributed to the Peter pictured in Paul's letters and in the narrative gospels. There is not a shred of historical evidence to support it (211, 213).

Again, this is from the pen of a white Christian scholar, so make sure you vent your anger in the right direction! Jude and II Peter are very poor writings for any-one who wants to make a case against Sodom, Gomorrah, gays, lesbians, or hell-fire. Their interpretation of Sodom's destruction is as far off the mark as east is to west! The writers of these "crude" works were merely parroting oral tradition that had been so changed by the time they got the story that the real reason for the city's destruction had long been lost.

The sad thing about the Sodom and Gomorrah story is that we have relied on this garbage in the New Testament as holy-inspired, which it ain't, to dog the shyt out of homosexuals! We read the Bible (especially the New Testament) as though it is a comprehensive historical account of first century Palestine. The New Testament isn't true historicity! The book is like opening one's eyes for a brief second and then going back to sleep.

How many preachers teach the history of first century Palestine and the his-tory of Bible compilation? Very few! These preachers get up in their pulpit on a Sunday morning and talk shyt against the homosexual. At the same time, many of them are eyeing some young, fine-ass sista! They're pushing up on your daughter and you're wondering why she doesn't want to go to church! Or they're somewhere stomping their wife in a parking lot—giving her the hard-bottom/*Stacey Adams* special! (Fuck the bad Rev. Thomas Weeks!) The fag and the dike have gotta die, but Rev. Chickenfoot can have all the pussy he wants 'cause he's doin' "de Lawd's work!" You should know that most of these preachers are just frontin' as men-of-the-cloth and haven't done any serious studies in the religion they profess! If they were truly called to preach THE WORD, they'd know that the things I'm breakin' off are true and you'd know they were true because you would've been taught THE TRUTH.

The Truth About Sodom & Gomorrah's Destruction.

Now let me explain why Sodom and Gomorrah was destroyed. First, it WAS NOT because they were homosexuals, rump-rangers, booty-bandits, browntowners, hershey-highwayers, or just plain ol' faggots. NO! Kill that idea from your mind! All that faggot stuff your dumb-ass preacher has taught you was a lie! Sodom and Gomorrah was destroyed because they were inhospitable, haughty, and arrogant! What? Yes! They lacked HOSPITALITY! What is hospitality? **The American Heritage Dictionary** defines hospitality as: *Cordial and generous reception of guests* (Berube et al., p.624). Hospitality? Yes, hospitality! In the Ancient Near East, being hospitable to the stranger was of the utmost importance and one of the greatest virtues. Some of you think I'm just makin' up this stuff! I hear you! You're saying, *"Why would God destroy those cities just because they had no manners!?"* I hear you! Now read some scholarship on the subject and then holla at me! **The Oxford Companion to the Bible** writes:

> [Hospitality is] one of the most highly praised virtues in antiquity [olden times] ... [it] was an unwritten law, and the stranger was regarded as divinely protected ... because the Israelites had been strangers in Egypt, they should show hospitality to strangers. It is therefore not surprising that people on occasion are rebuked for not being hospitable ... Hospitality is so highly regarded that in Isaiah 58:7 it is preferred to fasting ... Hospitality was equally important among the Greeks and Romans ... The New Testament accords extraordinary importance to hospitality. (Luke 10:29-37) Hospitality ... was a part of Jesus' teaching. (Coogan & Metzger, 292).

The Interpreter's Dictionary of the Bible writes this of Hospitality:

> Entertainment of a stranger as a guest; recognized as a sacred duty through-out the Mediterranean world, and more heartily and stringently kept than many a written law ... Hospitality was discharged more from fear and for protection than from generosity.... the host never knew when he himself would be dependent on others. The guest was treated with respect and honor and was provided with provender for his animals, water for his feet, rest, and a sumptuous feast. He enjoyed protection, even if he were an enemy, for three days and thirty-six hours after eating with the host (the time sustained by his food). Hospitality was to the Bedouin what almsgiving was to the later Jews ... (Buttrick et al., Vol. E-J, p.654).

James L. Kugel, in his book, **The Bible As It Was**, writes:

> Being stingy and inhospitable, especially to strangers, was no small matter. From ancient times, this had been considered a particularly grave fault. Indeed, the Sodomites' stinginess ... stood in sharp contrast to Abraham's behavior (189).

As we see, hospitality was a great virtue back then. This was the Sodomites' crime ... inhospitality, not homosexuality! Let me further prove it. Look at Ezekiel 16:49-50:

> ... this was the iniquity [sin] of thy sister Sodom, PRIDE, FULLNESS OF BREAD, and ABUNDANCE OF IDLENESS ... NEITHER DID SHE [Sodom] STRENGTHEN THE HAND OF THE POOR AND NEEDY [they were greedy and selfish] and THEY [Sodomites] WERE HAUGHTY [proud and vain to the point of arrogance].

See? That's right there in your Bible! You never saw Sodom like that, did you? Ezekiel never equated the sin of Sodom with homosexuality! He said that greed, arrogance, and pride were the culprits in Sodom's destruction. This was the real reason for God destroying those cities! The book of Ezekiel was written ca. 590 B.C.E. Do you feel what I'm sayin'? Those phony-ass books of the New Testament (II Peter & Jude) came along some 500-600 years later! Those books flip-da-script and made Sodom's sin homosexuality. A late tradition. Again, **The Bible As It Was** writes:

> According to this list [Ezekiel 16], it was primarily the Sodomites' pride and their failure to aid the poor amidst their own prosperity that caused God to

smite them ... As a result, a great many interpreters [including the author] read the story of Lot quite differently. He settled in a city of haughty, wealthy, but inhospitable and tightfisted people ... (Kugel187). [Interpreters] were equally perplexed about the city of Sodom. God destroyed it because of the terrible things that were being done there-but what exactly were those things? Strangely, the Genesis narrative, does not say. The men of Sodom are said to be "evil and very grave" (Gen. 13:13), and at one point God observes that the Sodomites' "sin is very grave" (Gen. 18:20), but that is all we are told (185).

Look at Jeremiah 23:14:

I have seen also in the prophets of Jerusalem an horrible thing: THEY COMMIT ADULTERY, and walk in lies, they strengthen the hand of evildoers, ... they are all of them unto me as SODOM and the inhabitants thereof as GOMORRAH.

What do you make of this scripture? If you don't see it let me let Professor Kugel tell you.

If God equated adulterers in Jerusalem to the people of Sodom, then it follows that the latter [the Sodomites] were no less guilty of adultery than of homosexual acts (185).

You got it now? Jeremiah says the prophets of Jerusalem are like Sodom because they are adulterous! To be adulterous there must be a union between a man and a woman who are married. So, at the very least, the Sodomites were adulterous as well as stingy and inhospitable. Jeremiah makes the connection that at least some of the Sodomites were heterosexual/married men else they couldn't be ADULTERERS! Duh! Here are some ancient references to Sodom. You tell me what their sin was, homosexuality or inhospitality!

You [God] burned with fire and brimstone the **arrogant** Sodomites, who were unseen in their vices, and you made them as example to posterity [future generations] (3 Maccabees 2:5) (187).

Others [the Sodomites] had refused to **receive strangers** when they came (Wisdom 19:14) (187).

The region of the Sodomites ... was laden with innumerable injustices, especially those arising from **gluttony** and **lust**.... The cause of this excess in licentiousness among the inhabitants [of Sodom] was the unfailing abundance of wealth, for, provided with deep soil and ample water, this region every year enjoyed a harvest of all manner of crops ... They threw off from their necks the law of nature by indulging in **strong drink, rich food, and forbidden forms of intercourse** (Philo, *Abraham* 134-135) (188).

Because of his **hospitality** and piety, Lot was saved from Sodom (I Clement 11:1)

Be not forgetful to entertain strangers [show hospitality]: for thereby some [Lot and the Sodomites] have entertained angels unawares (Hebrews 13:2).

As I've repeatedly stated, the Sodom and Gomorrah story is not about homosexuality as the New Testament suggests, but rather the total disregard for the Ancient Near Eastern custom of HOSPITALITY. **The Eerdmans Bible Dictionary** states:

God destroyed the city [Gomorrah] along with Sodom because of the wickedness of its inhabitants ... Sodom and Gomorrah thus became proverbial for wickedness and divine punishment ... while MANY TAKE THIS ACCOUNT TO BE A CONDEMNATION OF HOMOSEXUALITY, THE FOCUS OF DIVINE DISPLEASURE IS RATHER THE CITIZENS' DISREGARD FOR THE NEAR EASTERN PRACTICE OF HOSPITALITY (Myers et al., p.431).

You got it? The oldest understandings of this story had absolutely nothing to do with homosexuality! That is a New Testament Christian invention! Peter J. Gomes, Professor of Christian Morals at Harvard University writes, *"And lest we forget Sodom and Gomorrah, recall that the story is not about sexual perversion and homosexual practices. It is about INHOSPITALITY."*

By now you should be getting a totally different view of Sodom's destruction. I tell you again, it was about their inhospitality, not their ass-fuckin'! The Bible has playa-hated on the Sodomites because the Sodomites had-it-goin'-on in the wealth department (and the religion department as we shall soon see) and like most of us, when we get a little status and wealth, we become arrogant and high-minded and aloof. This is what happened to the Sodomites. God/ess hated that they were arrogant! God/ess hated the fact that they were dishonoring the ancient unwritten law of hospitality! He/She hated that shyt so much that He/She burned them all up! That's why Jesus said in the New Testament:

"And into whatsoever city or town ye shall enter, inquire in it who is worthy; and there abide [stay] till ye go thence [leave]. And when ye come into an house,

salute [respect, honor] it. And if the house be worthy [if they let you come in], let your peace come upon it: but if it be not worthy, let your peace return to you And whosoever shall not receive you [show hospitality by letting you stay in their house], nor hear your words, when ye depart out of that house or city, shake off the dust of your feet. Verily I say unto you, IT SHALL BE MORE TOLERABLE FOR THE LAND OF SODOM and GOMORRAH IN THE DAY OF JUDGMENT, THAN FOR THAT CITY" (Matthew 10:11-15).

How many times have we read these scriptures and had a different under-standing? Whenever we read Sodom and Gomorrah, our minds went straight to faggotsville! Yes it did! But Jesus wasn't talking about Sodom and Gomorrah in the context of ass-fuckin'! He used these cities to tell his disciples about the *HOS-PITALITY* they would and should receive and how to deal with a city or a house that was unwelcoming to them and their message. That's it! Jesus understood what a lot of these foot-shuffling, bumbling idiots who call themselves preachers, pastors, and reverends don't understand! Jesus told his disciples that Sodom and Gomorrah stood a better chance on JUDGMENT DAY than a city or house that dissed them! Jesus understood that *INHOSPITALITY* was far worse than a little ass-fuckin' or two women bumpin' uglies! Now it is time for you to understand it. Again, when Jesus spoke of Sodom and Gomorrah, he was not using these cit-ies as a place to demonstrate that God hates and kills faggots! He referred to these cities to show what happens when you disrespect and ill-treat the servants of God (or anybody for that matter). Jesus understood the story of Sodom and Gomor-rah, not as an act of God's wrath against homosexual practices, but as payback for an inhospitable, arrogant, and stingy people. He never once attached homosexu-ality to Sodom! So why do you "Christ-like" Christians teach and believe some-thing about this story that was totally unheard of to Jesus' ears? Jesus knew that Sodomites were homosexuals but he didn't diss their sexual orientation? No! So why do you? The reason he didn't is because he understood that their homosex-ual practices were linked to their spirituality and that they were practicing what "modern," "biased," scholars term as "male-cultic-temple-prostitution." But Jesus was totally unconcerned with their religious beliefs and homosexual practices. He only cared about how the disciples would be treated. All of this can be extrapo-lated from Matthew 10. Go back and peep it!

Matthew 10 proves that Jesus was much wiser than these preachers today who take the story out of its historical context. Sodom's problems were much bigger than a few gay men out to rape two angels. Sodom had the same problems that we face today in America. The Jews and the people of biblical times were racist, classist, capitalistic, *"What have you done for me lately?,"* *"I gots mine, you get yours,"* *"Me, Myself and I,"* sexist, misogynistic, and homophobic, just as America is today! Sodom was filled-to-the-rim in excesses and profligate in its wealth, just as America is today! The Sodomites looked at the homeless, the street-bums, and the indigents, just as we look at the homeless on the street-corner, as we push up in our Benzes and Beemers and Chrysler 300s and lock our doors and roll our windows up and look straight ahead so that we don't have to face our collective national guilt.... the homeless. Then we can inwardly justify their situation to make ourselves feel better about our own self-centeredness and selfishness. We are no better than the Sodomites! We 21st century, First World, heterosexual, new-jack-ass Christians, think that the homosexual is going to bust hell wide open. But let me tell all of you Christians something! Every time you ride by a homeless person on a street-corner, while reading his or her cardboard sign, *"Will Work For Food,"* *"Homeless, Can You Spare Any Change?, God Bless You,"* *"No Need To Lie. I Just Want A Beer,"* you are doing exactly what the Sodomites of Lot's day did! You are, first, being judgmental of their situation, arrogant, high-minded, haughty, and plain ol' inhospitable. You've got a hundred nickels in your purse or ashtray, but can't get up off of them! You need your spare change, right? Stingy! That's all you are! I hear you! *"I ain't givin' him my change! All he's gonna do is buy crack and booze wit' it!"* Um tellin' you now! Your reward will be greater than the fate of Sodom and Gomorrah! That's what Jesus said!

Sodomite Religion

Yes! These Sodomites or homosexuals were very spiritual beings! Three thousand years ago that's how they were livin'. I gotta keep it real fo' ya! Yes, in Sodom and Gomorrah the Sodomites were indeed haughty and arrogant and selfish and inhospitable ... in those cities. But elsewhere, they were normal law abiding citizens who just happened to be homosexual. They were very religious and spiritual. Not only were they spiritual, but also they had their own religious system that the Jews indulged in along with the Yahweh cult. Hold on! Let me prove it.

If you look closely at the scriptures, which deal with the Sodomites you will see a recurring theme. In the four passages of the Old Testament, which specifically address the Sodomites (I Kings 14:24; 15:12; 22:46, II Kings 23:7), it is very clear why they were hated and it wasn't because they were homosexuals either! It was because they worshipped other gods and influenced the Jews to do likewise. They had such great influence that they were even able to set up their idols in the temple of the Jews! They were profaning the temple and influencing Israel to their way of worshipping, according to the kings and the Levites. The

Levites were a jealous bunch because the Goddess cults and the Sodomite cult were kickin' some shyt that was appealing to the Jews! Go check their history! When the Levites wrote laws, it wasn't, *"I the Lord am a jealous God!"* It was, *"We the Levitical priests are jealous demagogues!"* So they used God's name to further their agenda to destroy Sodomite religion as well as Goddess religion. The Sodomites sexual preference was not the issue at hand. The problem with the Sodomites is that they helped defile the high places of the Jews' temple. Look at I Kings 15:11-13:

> And Asa did that which was right in the eyes of the Lord ... And he took away the Sodomites out of the land, and removed all the idols that his fathers [Jews] had made [in honoring Sodomite religion]. And also Maachah his mother, even he removed her from being the queen, because she had made an idol, and burnt it by the brook Kidron.

Ah-ha! Now the truth comes out! The Sodomites were removed out of the land because they had too much juice (power)! Even the queen was givin' props to the Sodomites! See? The Sodomites were condemned for their religious practices, not for their ass fuckin'! You need to know and understand that! The priest didn't give a shyt about homosexuality in-and-of-itself! The only reason they wrote laws against homosexuality is because it was rooted in a religious practice that the Jews found appealing. Can you believe that King Asa would dethrone his own mama?! What was it about Sodomite religion that was so intriguing to the Israelites?

When you study a little deeper you'll find out that the Sodomites were indeed a very religious bunch. They engaged in what modern, biased, ethnocentric scholars call "male cultic temple prostitution" or any combination of those names. The Sodomites, like the Goddess religions, viewed sex (in any form) as holy and sacred.

Sex was the ultimate show of worship for these people. And just as Israel was attached to Canaanite and Babylonian Goddess religions, those Israelites (heterosexual & homosexual) saw in the Sodomite religion something that was appealing to them that the Yahweh cult (their own religion) could not give them ... sexual gratification. The Sodomites attracted Israelite men who were inclined to a gay lifestyle but they also attracted heterosexuals like Asa's ex-queen mother.

To reiterate, the act of homosexuality is not what Israel, through their priests, saw as disgusting. Homosexuality was not on trial back then! The problem was that the Sodomites had their own religious system, which was attractive to Israel just as the Goddess religion was popular with Israel. The Levites had the arduous task of doggin' any religion that posed a threat to their belief system. I'm here to set the historical record straight! Just tell the plain ol' troot (truth)! Irie mon! Stop the madness being taught by these dumb-ass preachers! They don't know what the hell they're talkin' 'bout! Stop the homophobic ignorance coming from the Islands! Rasta bwoy, you've been spoon fed cultural garbage that has masqueraded as religious truth! Every scripture was written for a purpose and a reason. When you find out that you've been duped by some ignorant men who lived 3,000 years ago, admit that you've been taken for a ride. The biblical polemic (argument) against homosexuality is a religious hoax, perpetrated for the expressed purpose of keeping the ancient Israelites from worshipping the god of their choice! Yahweh (God) DID NOT write against homosexuality! The Jewish priests did! Everything written in the Bible IS NOT the truth! That's mythology you've believed. God/ess did not write against homosexuality no more than He/She wrote in favor of a rapist marrying the woman he raped! That's sexist bullshyt! (Read 'em and weep! Exodus 21:7-11, Numbers 31:7-18, Deuteronomy 20:10-14; 21:10-14; 22:23-24-28-29, Judges 21:10-24 ... Oh! These are books in that dusty family Bible at your mama's house with all the pictures of beautiful white people in them.)

All Scripture From God?

I know some of you don't like what you're reading because you've so thoroughly convinced that every word in the Bible is the truth—inspired—perfect—from God. I know the Bible says, *"All scripture is given by inspiration of God ..."* (II Timothy 3:16), but I say, *"Who wrote that?"* Who and what is II Timothy? Is he the brother of I Timothy? Let me digress for a moment and kill the myth that the Bible is a perfectly "inspired" book. To begin with, the book of II Timothy is said to be the work of St. Paul. This is a misnomer—a lie! I & II Timothy are what biblical scholars call "Deutero" and "Pseudo-Pauline" writings, which means "secondary" and/or "false." Paul DID NOT write II Timothy! Professor Burton L. Mack writes, *"Their attribution to Paul is clearly fictional, for their language, style, and thought are thoroughly un-Pauline"* (208). The book, *An Introduction To The Bible* writes, *"Scholars consensus attributes to Paul seven authentic writings: I Thessalonians, Philippians, Galatians, Philemon, I & II Corinthians, and Romans"* (Beasley et al., pg. 427). So, again, who wrote II Timothy and this "all scripture inspired" crap? To put it bluntly, II Timothy was not around during Jesus' or Paul's lifetimes! Professor Mack further states, *"They were not included by Marcion's list of Paul's letters (Ca. 140 C.E./[A.D.]), nor do they appear in Irenaeus' 'Against Heresies'"* (206). You got that? These books (I & II Timothy) didn't come on the Christian scene until some 120+ years after Jesus and Paul died! But again, the question needs to be answered! Who wrote these books? Answer? An anonymous second century gentile who was just a generation removed from paganism! That's who wrote these books! The scholar Davidson writes:

> We rest in the conclusion that the author of [I & II Timothy] was a Pauline Christian who lived at Rome in the first part of the second century ... Like many others of his day, the author chose the name [Timothy] of an apostle to give currency to his sentiments (Sunderland 152).

Yes! The Bible is an "inspired" work. But "inspiration" IS NOT a connotation for "perfection!" The Bible is not infallible (without error-perfect). In fact, the Bible never claims to be free from error! As a matter of fact, Jesus' own words contradict much of what had been written in the Torah (law=Bible). Jesus said, *"Ye have heard that it was said by them of old time, thou shalt not kill ... But I say unto you ... "* (Matthew 5:21-22, 27-28). J.T. Sunderland writes:

> Jesus could not have known of the infallibility of the Old Testament when he cited passage after passage from it, to contradict it and to command the opposite. The truth is, the doctrine of Bible infallibility, or inerrancy, as taught in the modern world, was unknown to the early Christian Church. It did not come into existence until the sixteenth and seventeenth centuries, and was not held by the earliest and greatest reformers—Luther, Calvin, Zwingli and their associates (265).

I'm walking you the long way home. To fully understand the biblical homophobic myth, we have to demystify the Bible and put what is written in its proper historical place. This essay is the demythologization of the Bible and its homophobic myth. Again, just because you read it in the Bible, doesn't make it so! Break down the ingredients in cigarettes and you'll have to agree that it's bad for your health, even though it is legal to smoke! The same can be said for the Bible on the reverse. The Bible says that homosexuals should be put to death, but upon closer examination, we see that the writers weren't upset at homosexuality. They were mad that homosexuality was linked to another culture's religious practice! Stop using the Sodom and Gomorrah story to dog gays and lesbians because you're taking it out of its historical context and distorting the truth of the story. Sodom and Gomorrah was no more about homosexuality than it was about heterosexuality. It was about unrighteousness by all the people of Sodom, including heterosexuals. This was about sin ... transgression of the law (I John 3:4). But hold up! Stop the presses! Remember, Christians don't live under the law. They live under grace. So what gives?

The Levites & the Sodomites

Deuteronomy 23:17 says, *"There shall be no whore of the daughters of Israel, nor a sodomite of the sons of Israel."* Okay, smarty-pants, what does this law mean? Most people would say that this is a prohibition against prostitution and homosexuality. This is God's law against hoes and faggots right? WRONG! This law has absolutely nothing to do with selling pussy or a man takin' a dick up his ass! Say what? That's right! This law is not about prostitution and homosexuality. It's not about any kind sex act. Well Master Khalil, would you please help me to understand? Of course! This law (Deut. 23:17) against the "whore" and the "Sodomite" has to do with a religious practice. This law was a prohibition for the Jews against practicing and worshipping Goddess and Sodomite religions. The Levites who wrote this law didn't give a damn about a man sleeping with a man, so long as it was purely a sex act and not a form of religious worship. If you study the first five books of the Bible (Genesis, Exodus, Leviticus, Numbers, Deuteronomy), commonly called the Torah (Law) or Pentateuch (Five Books), you will find NO PROHIBITION against a woman having sex with a woman. **The Interpreter's Dictionary of the Bible** writes, *"Lesbianism is not mentioned in the OT [Old Testament], but is condemned with male homosexuality in the NT [New Testament] (Rom. 1:26-27; Gal. 5:19-20 ... "* (Crim et al., p. 819). You got it? In other words, the Jewish priests of the Old Testament felt no need to write against sistas bumpin' uglies, and believe me, it was goin' on! There is no law against lesbianism in the Old Testament! And guess what else? There isn't a prohibition against a man having sex with his daughter or his grandmother in the Old Testament! Find it! There are laws about a man fuckin' his female relatives, but that's it. This proves that the Levites ulterior motive had profound socio-religious overtones. They weren't too concerned about biology and genetic DNA composition. It proves that the Jewish priests' main reason for getting into folk's bedrooms was rooted in a religious practice, not a sexual practice, else they would have written a law for lesbians and made sure that they covered all of the unholy and incestuous unions, like father/daughter sex (which isn't condemned either).

The Levites saw the Goddess religion as "whores," thus writing the law as such. It was customary to give an alm or token to the woman with whom the man was going to have sex with, but, mind you, in their way of thinking, it wasn't sex for the sake of sex, but rather the ultimate show of religious devotion. Having sex is how these people showed their love to their god. Understand how these people were livin'. We can't judge that! **The Interpreter's Dictionary of the Bible** says, *"The law of Deuteronomy [23:17 whore & Sodomite] prohibits the practice of CULT PROSTITUTION ... "* (Buttrick et al., Vol. K-Q, p.933). See?! CULT PROSTITUTION! CULT! CULT! CULT! You do know what a cult is, don't you? **The American Heritage Dictionary** defines CULT as, *"A system or community of religious worship and ritual ... "* (Berube et al., p.348). How ya gonna call a peoples' religious beliefs and practices "whores" and "prostitutes" just because they run contrary to your pseudo-morality of the 21st Century?" The Levites wrote, *"There shall be no WHORE of the daughters of Israel, nor a SODOMITE of the sons of Israel,"* which shows an ethnocentric subjectivity (a bias) on their part by the use of the words "whore" and "sodomite" to describe a religious practice that they (the Levites) deemed disgusting. They intentionally and purposefully used negative words to describe the Sodomite's and the Goddess religion to mislead the people 3,000 years ago and to mislead you today! The Levites worst fear was seeing their own people convert to Sodomite and Goddess religion! So they used the *"Boogie Man"* approach to scare the people out of practicing foreign religions, but it didn't work. Actually, the *"Boogie Man"* approach works better today than it did for the original hearers of the Jewish Law. We, today, are scared shitless to search elsewhere for our salvation! We, today, are scared shitless to read the Qu'ran or the Vedas for fear that we're going to hell if we acknowledge these scriptures as sacred! Most of us will keep our kindergarten mentality when it comes to our religious beliefs (even after receiving a Ph.D. in Physics) because we have been "BOOGIE-MATIZED" (hypnotized) by our preacher and our particular brand of Christianity. You've heard them say, *"Don't question God!"* or *"You shouldn't question God!"* Keep on believing that homosexuality is bad! Keep on believing that the "whore" and the "Sodomite" were prostitutes and ass-fuckers! Keep on believing that bogus bullshyt! And while you believe that garbage, scholarship speaks loud and clear! **The Eerdmans Bible Dictionary** writes this of "cult prostitute":

Personnel associated with pagan temples for the purpose of ritual [religious] intercourse, generally to appease the gods and ensure fertility. According to Deut.23:17 [the scripture I just quoted] the Israelites were forbidden to engage in cultic [religious] prostitution, with either male or female prostitutes, as encouraged in the worship among some of the neighboring nations. That the Israelites could not resist yielding to such temptation is evident from I Kings, ... II Kings 23:7 even mentions rooms ("houses") to accommodate cult prostitutes in the temple at Jerusalem. (Myers et al., p.247).

The Oxford Companion to the Bible writes this of prostitution:

> It is widely assumed that some form of "sacred" or "cultic prostitution" characterized Canaanite religion; however, the LANGUAGE OF PROSTITUTION IS NEVER USED TO DESCRIBE CULTIC OFFICES OR ACTIVITIES IN ANCIENT NEAR EASTERN TEXTS outside the Bible's polemical [argumentative] usage. The Hebrew term sometimes rendered "sacred prostitute," qedesa, simply means, "consecrated (person)." Association with prostitution, or sexual activity of any sort, is inferred from biblical contexts and HAS NO PARALLEL IN EXTRA-BIBLICAL TEXTS (Metzger & Coogan, 624).

You got it? This so-called "Cultic Prostitution" is what modern-day, Christian, Bible-based scholars called the Sodomite's and the Goddess religion's practice. It is not accurate and does not allow us to fully understand the way they believed. "Prostitute" and "whore" are strictly biblical language, finding no place in other sacred writings of the Ancient Near East. The Levites use of this negative language was supposed to keep Israel from practicing foreign religions. The Sodomite and the Goddess religions didn't view themselves as "hoes" and "faggots" like we've interpreted their actions. Western-white-Christian scholars have distorted the very meaning of a holy and righteous practice that these people engaged in! That's just like non-Christians teaching that Christians are polytheists (many god worshippers) because they believe in something called the Trinity or the Triune or the Three-In-One, Father, Son, Holy Spirit/Ghost. A true Christian will tell you straight-up, "I believe in One God! These three are one!" Yeah, right!

So the Levites wrote Deut.23:17 to try and keep Israel from Goddess and Sodomite religion, not to keep them from sellin' pussy and takin' it (dick) up the ass! That's a revelation don't you think? I know many have read this scripture and saw hoes and fags. Yes we did! The so-called law against homosexuality is in Leviticus 18:22 which says, *"If a man also lie with mankind, as he lieth with a woman, both shall be put to death ..."* Why? Because there is something inherently wrong with homosexuality? No! Because sex between two men or two women is nasty, gross, and disgusting? No! Is that why the Levites felt the need to write against the practice? Hell naw! It is quite evident when you study their history that the polemic against homosexuality has its roots in Israel's worship of Sodomite and Goddess religions. This is the main reason that homosexuality became sinful—in the eyes of the Jewish priests who forged God's Name on their sacred writings, which we've been cosigning for the last 3,000 years.

Sodomites & Cult Prostitution

The prohibition against homosexuality is directly related to the Goddess and Sodomite cults that proliferated in the Ancient Near East. But here again, the Goddess worshippers and the Sodomites were not "prostitutes" as we understand prostitution today. In their language they were called the "Qades" or "holy/sacred" men. That's a far cry from being a prostitute! We need to stop thinking from our "Western" (white) mind-set and place ourselves within their culture. When we do this, the Sodomites were holy, good, reverent, and respectful people. Any use of the word "prostitute" dismisses the true essence of the Qades (Sodomites) and heaps on them a negative connotation, thereby misleading the reader. This is what the Bible (through our preachers) has done. Merlin Stone, author of **When God Was A Woman** says, *"... the word 'prostitute' entirely distorts the very meaning of the ancient custom [of the Sodomites and the Goddess religions] ..." (157).* To put this puppy to bed, read what **The Eerdmans Bible Dictionary** has to say on this subject.

> Of far greater concern to the Israelites was the practice of cultic prostitution common among the non-Israelite religions ... particularly that of the Canaanite fertility goddess Asarte. Both men (Deut. 23:[17]18 "sodomite," male prostitute) and women (qedesa or [qadishtu] "consecrated women") dedicated their lives to the deity, performing sexual acts with worshippers so as to encourage the deified forces of nature to imitate them and thus guarantee continued productivity and prosperity. Cultic prostitution was specifically prohibited in the Hebrew faith ... Nevertheless, many [Israelites] gave in to non-Israelite influences, participating in foreign rites (I Kings 14:24) and even introducing prostitution into the Israelite cult (e.g. I Kgs. 22:38, 2 Kgs. 23:7, Jer. 2:20, Hos.4:13-14) (Myers et al., p.462-63).

So there you have it! These Qades (Sodomites) and Qadishtu (Whores) weren't just fuckin' for the sake of fuckin'! They believed that sex would ensure fertility (which it did) from the gods and the goddesses. But even more important to their character is that they WERE NOT PROSTITUTES, FAGGOTS AND WHORES! They were holy men and sanctified women! Do you understand that?

Their concept of sex was 180 degrees in difference that our "Western" concept of sex and it is very evident in the scholars' erroneous use of the word "prostitute" to describe these people's religious practices. The so-called whore and the homosexual had-it-goin'-on so tough that the Israelites found themselves indulging in worshipping the Sodomite and the so-called whore's religion! This is the REAL

REASON why God supposedly (and the Levites) forbids homosexuality for the Israelites! Not because homosexuality (in-and-of-itself) is bad, but because it caused Israel to turn from their God Yahweh! That's why homosexuality was condemned! That is the truth, which is forbidden to be taught in the Christian church. The Christian argument against homosexuality is contradictory in that they quote Jewish Law and cite a Jewish story while they trash Jewish law (for Grace) while adopting a Jewish story.

Interesting revelation huh? I've been tryin' to tell ya you've been taught a lie! The bottom-line is that if homosexuality were not so closely aligned with so-called "cultic prostitution" it would not have been an issue for the Levites and therefore permissible to engage in. The Israelites set up the whole sex game 3,000 years ago and we are still caught up in it today! Imagine how we might view homosexuality today had not the Levites had to deal with it? Would we be calling homosexuals "fags," "punks," "queers," and "dikes" if the Bible hadn't went on an overt homophobic campaign first? From the Old Testament's point of view, homosexuality is only bad because it caused Israel to worship other gods. This is clearly the reason for the condemnation of homosexuality.

We're always hearing some ig-nant assed Christian on a talk show, not quoting the Bible, but telling us what the Bible supposedly says about homosexuality. They want us to believe that they know what the phuck they're talkin' about when, in actuality, they're just parroting some shyt they think they heard Bro. Preacher say in church. Do they know that the Sodomites were a bona fide religion back then and not just a bunch of ass-fuckers? Hell naw! Do they know that those so-called prostitutes served the needs of the temple, even the Jews' Temple at Jerusalem and that if they were alive today they would be seen and viewed as we view Mother Teresa?

Christian Law?

Thus far, all that you've read is Old Testament Jewish Law. But this is not the Christian way. Remember, "grace" not "law." So when Christians speak of "God's Law" being against homosexuality they're contradicting their own doctrine of grace. Now either Christians don't really believe in this "faith and grace" stuff that they purport or they're being contradictory and hypocritical. If you tell a Christian that Jesus did not come to abrogate (destroy) the Law, you will have a major argument on your hands. They'll argue that we live by faith through the grace of Jesus Christ. That is the New Covenant (agreement). The law is no longer in effect because Jesus died as a sacrificial lamb for the sins of the world.

This belief is fundamental to the faith. Folks like Augustine and Luther beat all hell out of this exact point!

So why do Christians still feel the need to resort to Old Testament Law to argue against homosexuality? It is contradictory, paradoxical, and hypocritical! All-of-a-sudden the story of Sodom and Gomorrah becomes so damned relevant and the focal point for dissin' homosexuals! All-of-a-sudden, Levitical Law is being cited by Christians as the moral pretext for the condemnation of gays and lesbians! Pickin' and choosin' which laws are relevant and which aren't! That's what these two-faced Christians have done. The Law is dead but then they turn around and use the Old Testament Law to condemn homosexuality. Well what about the rest of the Law?!

There are 613 laws, statutes, judgments, and commandments in the Old Testament. Why is it that only the laws your religion "can get with" are used? You say God's Word is against homosexuality while eating a big greasy pork sammich! Why do you eat bacon, pork sausages and chitlins? Did you know that the Bible has a prohibition against eating pork, lobster, shrimp, crabs, oysters, squid, octopus (calamari), and catfish? (Go read Leviticus 11) Oooh boy! I sure love a plate of catfish and spaghetti! Yeah, that's some down-home eatin'! Read Leviticus 11:7-8 where God says, "Don't eat pork, don't touch pork!" You fuckin' hypocrite you! You are the one Jesus was talkin' about! Come on! Justify why you do the things you do when it comes to your religious beliefs! I know! You run over to the New Testament and quote some bullshyt scripture, *"Da Lawd made everything good."* And then you go over to Acts 15 where God supposedly did away with "unlawful" foods at the infamous Council of Jerusalem. The Jerusalem Church supposedly made some compromises for the gentiles. They teach you where Jesus supposedly said, *"Not that which goeth into a mouth defileth a man, but that which cometh out of the mouth, this defileth a man"* (Matthew 15:11). Then, your preacher tells you that gentiles (everybody except a Jew, i.e. Christians) were free from circumcision and free to eat whatever meats, so long as they weren't strangled or offered to idols. I got 'em down pat!

You say you believe in the Ten Commandments but you go to church on Sunday? You say you believe in the Ten Commandments but have a white picture (graven image) of Jesus on your wall, calling him "god" and equal to the Father? But, historically speaking, Jesus was a practicing Jew/Israelite who followed the dietary laws of the Old Testament and taught no such-a thing as the abolishment of the Law! Jesus never ate a ham sammich! Acts 15 was the New Testament compromise on behalf of the Jerusalem Church headed by James,

Peter, and John to allow those gentile believers who wanted to follow Jesus (and Paul), but couldn't or didn't want the stringency of the Jewish law.

What I'm tryin' to show you is that this is hogwash the Christian church has taught about homosexuality being against God's Law. It's pure pooh-pooh! How can it be against God's Law when Christians say they don't live under the Law? Maybe they should say they don't live under most of God's Laws (like eating pork and profaning the Sabbath) with the exception of homosexuality and a few other trivial laws. If the Christian believes in the dogma of grace and faith, are not gays and lesbians part of that grace? Since we live under grace, homosexuals should receive the same salvific opportunity and go to the same heaven as any heterosexual. St. John 3:16 says, *"Whosoever believeth in him … shall have everlasting life."* The operative word here is WHOSOEVER! It doesn't say whosoever if you're white, black, gay, straight, Republican, Democrat, Catholic, or Baptist! Just believe in Jesus and you shall see paradise!

For the enlightened, educated, liberal, and freethinking mind, homosexuality is not an issue. Let adults do whatever they want behind closed doors. It pisses me off when I see these no-brainers on TV who make catchy little phrases like, *"God created Adam and Eve, not Adam and Steve!"* No wonder America is so phucked up! This is the kind of profound insight we have when dealing with people's lives! The question of homosexuality is reduced to some nursery school Mother Goose rhyme shyt, from the mouths of supposedly freethinking, intelligent adults! None of these audience members or their guests knows the Bible but feels free to misquote and take out of historical context anything that remotely disses homosexuality. Homosexuality is as old as humankind and here we are in 2007-08 still debating the nature/nurture/biochemical/physiological reasons for homosexuality! When are we going to finally accept the fact that homosexuality is, in fact, NATURAL! It is a NATURAL part of human sexuality.

The Anus Argument

Some have argued that homosexuality is "not natural" because the anus (ass hole/ rectum) wasn't created for penetration. Its only function is for defecating (taking a dump/doo-dooing). It is for excretion only! I disrespectfully disagree. Why? If we're going to use this argument (the *"Anus Argument"*), then we should apply that to *Kissing, Sucking Breasts, Anal Sex* (between a man and a woman), *Fellatio* (dick sucking), *Cunnilingus* (pussy eating), *Noncoital Orgasm* (masturbation), *Coitus Interruptus* (when a man pulls out during sex and ejaculates on a woman's breasts and body. Some call it a pearlneckless=sperm on a woman's neck), *Sadomasochism* (S&M=spankings, chains, whips), *Bondage* (being tied up or handcuffed while causing sexual stimulation), *Voyeurism* (watching others having sex), *Exhibitionism* (getting off on letting others watch you having sex), *Roll Playing/Fantasies*, and last but not least, *"Swallowing."* (Women who like to ingest sperm). If homosexuality/man on man anal sex is not "natural," how much more "unnatural" is a woman who likes to swallow a man's sperm? Is that "natural?" According to their argument, NO! Sperm was meant for procreation! ... To make babies! But many heterosexual women love to taste their man's cum. What about kissing? By their argument kissing is not "natural" because the mouth was created for eating and speaking, and secondarily, for breathing. What purpose does a man and a woman sticking their tongues in each other's mouths serve? That ain't "natural!" According to the *"Anus Argument,"* a woman's breasts are for one purpose ... to give milk to a baby, not for a man to enjoy! This too would be an "unnatural" use of a woman's breasts.

According to the *"Anus Argument,"* fellatio would be an "unnatural" act. The male penis is for urine excretion and sex ... to piss and make a baby, not for a woman to lick and suck on. But how many heterosexual men like having their penis sucked? Perhaps 99.99999999999999%?! *(I would argue 100%, but I know there's some freak out there that is repulsed by a woman rapping her luscious lips around the head of his cock! To not want this! Now that's unnatural! I've also heard of men who would never let their girlfriend or wife suck dick because they somehow feel that they're sucking their own Johnson! How demented! But they'll still let some skank in the street go down on them.)* And how many heterosexual women indulge in this "unnatural" act of wrapping their lips around a man's penis? See how silly and contradictory it is for the heterosexual to say that a man should not put his penis in another man's rectum because it is "unnatural," and use the bogus argument of the rectum's purpose, yet the heterosexual contradicts his own *"Anus Argument"* by engaging in forms of sex that are, according to their own argument, "unnatural?"

Again, according to the, *"Anus Argument,"* cunnilingus would be an "unnatural" act. What purpose does it serve for a man to put his face between a woman's legs and taste her fluids? The tongue/mouth was made for tasting food, speaking and breathing. Not to be inserted into a woman's vagina! I ain't never met a woman that didn't want me to go down on her because it was "unnatural!" (Well, maybe once ... frigid bytch!) I guess its okay for the heterosexual male to practice the "unnatural" act of *cunnilingus*, but ass fuckin' has got to go!

What about *noncoital orgasm*? Masturbation! Is that unnatural? What's its purpose? Most men and women have masturbated to a sleaze magazine or a porno. Many of you all have dildoes and blow-up dolls. Sometimes we just wanna be with our self and work things out. *(That's what I hear 'cause I've never mastur-bated. I'm trying to sell beachfront property in Nebraska!)* How about *coitus inter-ruptus*? Isn't it unnatural for a man to pull out during orgasm and allow his seed to splash all over his woman's face, mouth, breasts, and stomach? Shouldn't he be trying to make a baby?

How many heterosexual couples have tried *anal sex?* It may not be for every-one, but many men have desired to fuck their woman up the ass. And many het-erosexuals practice anal sex while they are staunch opponents of the gay lifestyle. It's natural for a man to put his dick up a woman's ass but not another man's? Hmmm? Hypocrisy!

Do you REALLY want me to "keep it real?" Okay! What's the #1 all-Ameri-can heterosexual male fantasy? ... Two women in bed at the same time, a three-some, a *ménage a trois,* right? Of course! It is our ultimate fantasy! We don't just want to screw two women. We want to see these two women screw each other! Oh yes we do! We don't mind homosexual activity between two women because it is so erotic and beautiful and passionate the way they interact with one another. We heterosexual men like that shyt! I ain't NEVER met a straight man that didn't like girl-on-girl action! If most of our wives/girlfriends all-of-a-sudden came home and announced that she wanted you to screw her very curvaceous coworker while she licked her nappy dugout (vagina), you'd start pre-cumming when the doorbell rang! Whaaaat? You can hardly find a porno video where there isn't a scene where two women are licking each other's poonanny. Most of the mainstream pornographic magazines that you can buy in porno shops and conve-nient stores like *"Club," "Black Sista," "Black Tail," "Player," "Hustler," "Genesis," "Swank," "Gent," "High Society," "Chic,"* and *"Oui,"* have spreads of two women gettin' freak-nasty *(I've never personally viewed any of these magazines because I'm too busy building a spaceship in my backyard).* These porno magazines cater to a heterosexual male audience. Why do they think a male heterosexual audience is turned on by homosexuality between two women? Could it be that heterosexual men who diss gays are not truly homophobic, but rather pseudo-homophobes? ... Homophobes with stipulations. Homophobes with an asterisk*? That is, homophobes when it comes to male-on-male relationships. This must be the case! If you go to strip clubs, the biggest audience response happens as a result of two women on stage gyrating their bodies on each other and rubbing baby-oil all over each other. *(Again, I have to admit that I've never been to a strip club because that darn buffalo I bought still hasn't learned how to skate!)* How about *Jerry Springer?* The men in the audience love it when lipstick lesbians start kissing each other. In unison they chant, *"We love lesbians! We love lesbians! We love lesbians!"*

They go bananas! Why do we enjoy watching two women get-it-on but are repulsed at the sight of two men making love? We live in a society where lesbianism is an acceptable sexual behavior for heterosexual men. It doesn't matter how much "jesus" we claim to have in us, somewhere in our past, we were exposed to lesbianism and we enjoyed watching two women do their thing. Face it heterosexual men, we are some phuckin' hypocrites! Again, it shows that the *"Anus Argument"* is flawed in its conception and contradictory in its application. We say anal sex between two men is not natural but we desire to fuck our woman in the ass! Heterosexual distaste to homosexuality is really homosexuality between two men, not two women and that's the truth, Ruth!

We won't even go into S&M, Bondage and the rest of our freaky get-offs. Every heterosexual, male and female, who has had sex has engaged in some form of unnatural sex according to the *"Anus Argument."*

The bottom-line is that there is no such thing as an unnatural sex act between two consenting adults, be they heterosexual, homosexual or bisexual. The only exceptions would be incest (sex with family members), pedophilia (sex with children), and bestiality (sex with animals). So when these heterosexuals come on TV and use the *"Anus Argument,"* saying that it's unnatural for two men to have sex, you can see their very hypocritical argument. When they parrot their little homophobic nursery rhyme, *"God created Adam and Eve, not Adam and Steve!,"* you can see them for what they are … contradictory, silly, closed-minded, Christian brainwashed, uninformed, homophobic, scripturally illiterate, wannabe theologians who have no clue what the Bible's polemic (argument) against homosexuality was really about. All of what we say negative about homosexuals is just some bullshyt parroting from bigoted parents and friends and ignorant homophobic dumb-dog preachers.

The Hip-Hop/rap world is definitely into homosexuality … homosexuality between women … lesbianism. *Vibe* magazine (considered an authority on Hip-Hop culture) has a spread in its' June 2001 issue (featuring Missy "Misdemeanor" Elliot on the cover) of a jet-black sista and a white chick wearing bikinis and touching one another in a very sexually suggestive way. The title of the piece is called, *"Park and Ride: What a male fantasy: Two fast Women In Fast Cars."* Heterosexual men are turned on by women making out! That's the message of the ad … two chicks in fast cars will sell cars to men.

And check out these rap/R&B videos! *(*I refer to these videos because this essay was written when these videos were hot, but there are many examples today that are of the same thematic model).* From *Mystikal's, "Shake Ya Ass"* and *"Dangerous" where* he has scantily clad black women in bikinis, thongs, G-strings, and topless gyrating their hips, simulating sex with one another. This is lesbianism on the D/L that sells the record. Accepted homosexuality between women! An old video like *Sisqo's, "The Thong Song."* There's one scene where two women lay on the beach, one laying flat on her stomach while the other woman is leaning over her, sensuously rubbing her body. This is simulated lesbianism on the low-low, but it's aiiight 'cause it's two women! Check out *Outkast's* video, *"So Fresh, So Clean."* There's a scene where *Andre 3000* turns around and catches two women kissing mouth to mouth and turns and faces the camera, not with disapproval of their homosexual foreplay, but approving like, *"Oh shit! Two freaks in da house!"* Other examples of simulated homosexual foreplay between women can be seen in *Jay-Z's, "Big Pimpin'"* video and *Nas'/QueensBridge Finest/Braveheart, "Oochie Wally."* Check Nelly's, Lil Wayne's & Baby's, ... The list goes on and on. Rap videos are full of Homo-eroticism/foreplay between women. It is the acceptance of homosexual innuendo/foreplay between black women that drives and sells rap music to the consumer. The only way images of black women dancing and touching one another in these videos can appear is that they have mainstream heterosexual male acceptance, and I assure you, they do. But let *Mary J. Blige, Foxy Brown,* or *Lil Kim* come out with a video exhibiting a bunch of men in thongs dancing in front of each other with seductive looks for each other spewed across their faces with hard-ons and we'd have a riot! *MTV* would never allow it to air because we are not ready for that kind of sexuality ... man on man simulated Homo-eroticism.

Homophobia is as ignorant as Negrophobia (fear of black people). Whether we see signs of homophobia on TV or hear it on our favorite CD, it is still ignorance. Rappers are famous for using homophobic language in their music. Rappers like this white boy Eminem exhibit their ignorance by dissin' gays and then he has the nerve to perform with Mr. Gay himself, Elton John. What was that shyt about? Eminem has dissed women, gays and his mama! And the shameful thing about Eminem is that hip-hoppers endorse him because he's connected to Dr. Dre and can rap (for a white boy) and "acts" black. Personally, I don't trust no white muthafucka that would diss his own mama on wax! Black rappers have never dissed their mamas. That shyt is unacceptable in black culture. I don't care if your mama was the biggest ho on earth! A nicca will phuck you up for talkin' 'bout his mama! Playin' da dozens has gotten many-a nicca a beat down. Even Tupac rapped, *"and even as a crack fiend, mama, you always was a black queen ..."* L.L. Cool J rapped, *"Mama said knock you out!"* How the phuck ya gonna diss the womb from whence you came?! What did Eminem's mama do so bad that he had to diss her on his CD? So what if she had a drug problem! So did Tupac's mama and many of our black mamas! So what if he came from a dysfunctional home! Guess what? I did too! But my mama died at 42 years old! ... When I was still a phuckin' kid! I'd gladly take the live dysfunctional home with my live mama over the dead perfect home without her! Eminem shows us that no matter how much "hip-hop," "nigga," "soul," "credibility by being connected to Dr. Dre," and "black culture" he's been exposed to, he's still a white man, oblivious to what black people hold dearly—our mamas, masquerading as the "Elvis" of hip-hop, using the genre to diss gays, women, and his own mama in the name of artistic freedom! Let's REALLY keep it real! The only reason Eminem doesn't use the word "nigger" (as a racist epithet) or "nigga" (as a term of endearment) in his music is because black America ain't ready for that shyt! Black America will never accept a white person using the "N word" in their music in the spirit of "artistic freedom." No amount of association with Dr. Dre or Fiddy will keep Eminem from getting his ass kicked the minute he steps into the 'hood! Niccas will bum-rush the stage the minute "nigga" comes out of his mouth! Eminem knows this! He knows that it is not socially acceptable or politically correct for him to use the word nigga/nigger. I'm sure that Dre and company has already advised him of the grave error of using nigger. But because gays and lesbians are perceived as not having the mentality and the fire and the zest and the straight-up "I'll kick your muthafuckin' ass" mentality that black folk have when confronted by a white person using the "N word," he feels comfortable in calling out "faggots." To be gay is to be weak, they think. But um tellin' you! Niccas better peep game 'cause sooner or later (when Eminem's record sales start slipping and he needs a new shtick or shocker), this white boy is gonna come outta pocket and start calling black people niggers to sell more records. As far as calling out gays, Eminem better watch his back 'cause they got some niccas and some Eses' out here calling themselves "Homo-Thugs" and "Gayngstas" that will fuck him up. Black/Hispanic, thug, gangstas, that happen to be homosexual, that don't fit the stereotype of the soft feminine male. There's a whole subculture of gay/lesbian/transgender hip-hop heads, which have great stories to tell. And it's time to hear them! Times a changin'!

Homosexuality In History

When we look at homosexuality in history we see that it has always existed. There never was a time in recorded human history that the idea of two men or two women having sex did not exist. Homosexuality is as natural to the human condition as disease, death, war, the wheel, and sliced bread! No matter what the cultural norms and religious beliefs of a nation are, homosexuality still exists. I will admit that it seems to be more prevalent in certain countries and dormant in others. But this may in part be due to the severity of the law against homosexuality more so than people not wanting to engage in that lifestyle. As stated in the introduction, some afrocentric thinkers tend to want to believe that homosexuality is a perversion created by the white man—that homosexuality is absent on the continent of Africa—wishful thinking!

Certainly, the Christian Church, over the centuries has been very aware of the practice of homosexuality. Homosexuality is as akin to the Catholic Church as pedophilia and abstinence. The Vatican continues to take a hard-line stance against homosexuality while its priests, the world over, engage in fornication, pedophilia, sexual harassment, molestation, and homosexuality. Recently, young men and women have come out of the woodwork, describing vivid memories of their Catholic Church father sexually abusing them. These priests are then sent to other parishes after their deviant behavior is found out. Most of them are never punished and the Vatican sweeps it under the rug! Shame on them!

In a community where there are no women, homosexuality will become the norm. It's also true for a community without men. And so it is with monasteries, nunneries, and prisons. The need for sexual release/gratification is stronger that any "will" we may have towards abstinence. Abstinence is a trained/learned behavior. It is not natural. Sex is a biological response that the body craves just like food. The humanistic psychologist Abraham Maslow, in his *Hierarchy of Needs,* says that humans first strive to meet their most basest/primitive needs, which are our physiological needs. These would include hunger, thirst, elimination, warmth, fatigue, pain avoidance, and SEXUAL RELEASE (Rathus 307). This is the first rung of the ladder. After these needs are met, then we worry about safety, love and belongingness, esteem, and self-actualization needs. But food, drink and sex are a number one priority!

Imagine if what Maslow is saying is the gospel truth and then we, as a society, make it a capital offense for homosexuals to have sex. Their "basest" need would go unmet! And even closer to home, what happens to these monks and priests, who take a vow of celibacy in light of Maslow's Hierarchy? It is a foregone conclusion that some will stray from their vows and take on deviant sexual behaviors with our children or become homosexual.

This is what happened during the Middle Ages in the Catholic Church. Many monks, priests, bishops, popes, and kings were homosexual. And then there were many priests who had concubines (wives) on the "low-low" (in secret) and children from these women but still carried the party-line celibacy lie.

I am reminded of a notorious homosexual king named Edward II, the son-in-law of that notoriously evil King Philip IV of France. Although married, Edward wanted no parts of his wife. He was love struck by a young knight and they carried on a long-standing open homosexual relationship. Edward, his father-in-law King Philip IV, and the puppet pope Clement V conspired and destroyed a group of Christian knights/monks called the Knights Templars on Friday, October 13, 1307. That's where we get this unlucky number thirteen and Friday the 13th from. The Knights Templars were accused of … guess what? … homosexual practices among other things. Most of the charges were bogus 'cause King Edward II was a known homosexual and it didn't seem to affect his relationship with his daddy-in-law.

Another grand homosexual that graced the English throne was King James I, who "authorized" the writing of the most widely read Bible in the world, the King James Bible, which is probably the one most of us grew up with. Hmmm? That's right! If you read the "King James" version of the Bible you are reading something that a "faggot" legislated! The very Bible that some of us use to burn gays and lesbians came into existence at the behest of a homosexual!

Had King James known that folks would one day be trippin' on his lifestyle he might've ordered those scholars to remove all anti-homosexual language from the Bible. Then where would you be? Just as other things were purged from the Bible (like the Secret Gospel of Mark … go study it), the Sodom and Gomorrah story could have been rewritten and any negative talk about the Sodomites could have been purged from your "inspired scriptures." In our madness to make a case against homosexuality we fail to realize that the most popular version of the Bible (the King James Version 1611) was written under the auspices and direction of a homosexual!

Famous Homosexuals

As stated, homosexuality is as old as man/woman himself/herself. Some of the most famous people in history who have made an impact in our lives, either directly or indirectly have been gay or lesbian. According to the book, **The Gay 100,** these would include Socrates, Alexander the Great, Leonardo da Vinci, Augustine (the great Christian church father), Shakespeare, Michelangelo, Tchaikovsky, King David & Jonathan, Francis Bacon, Julius Caesar, Richard "the Lionhearted," King William III, Hafiz the poet, Byron, Walt Whitman, Oscar Wilde, Susan B. Anthony, Gertrude Stein, Virginia Woolf, Andy Warhol, James Baldwin, Eleanor Roosevelt, Nijinski, Tennessee Williams, Florence Nightingale, Barney Frank, Bayard Rustin, Rock Hudson, Liberace, Allen Ginsberg, Marlene Dietrich, Martina Navratilova, Ma Rainey, Bessie Smith, Nureyev, Freddie Mercury, Lawrence of Arabia, and Madonna (Russell 1).

Look at what these homosexuals have given the world! Look at the good, the joy, the intelligence, the inspiration, and the talent that homosexuals have given to the world. Shakespeare is considered by many to be the greatest poet that ever lived! A gay man! Michelangelo, one of the greatest artists to ever paint and the painter of the ceiling of the Sistine Chapel where the pope prays! Another gay man! Augustine ... SAINT AUGUSTINE, the African Church father who is still revered and venerated as a great theologian of the Christian church who was made a saint! A homosexual saint! Bayard Rustin, one of the figures behind the historic "March on Washington, 1963." Homosexual! James Baldwin, a great (black) American, one of our literary giants! If you don't know what these famous people have given humanity, I suggest you study them and try to accomplish half of what they've done and stop worrying about who a homosexual is sleeping with! If some of us had it our way, these people would be stoned to death! Thank God that the barbarity of the Bible is not in effect!

Yes, the Bible is barbaric! This same Bible that many of us hold as our "moral guide" has some of the most sexually perverted and raunchy stories in it! Have you read it lately? The scandals in it would even make the Greeks and the Romans blush with shame! Look at these HETEROSEXUALS at work! Did not Abraham marry Sarah, his half-sister (incest) (Genesis 20:12)? Did not Nahor marry his brother's daughter, his niece Milcah (incest) (Genesis 11:27-29)? Did not Lot fuck his two daughters and impregnate them, making himself the daddy and the granddaddy (ugh! incest) (Genesis 19;36-38)? Sounds like some "Color Purple" shyt, don't it? What about Jacob marrying two sisters who were his first cousins (Genesis 29:10-28)? What about David committing adultery with Bathsheba and then falling in lust with the pussy and having her husband Uriah put on the front line in a war to become "cannon fodder" and be killed (II Sam. 11:1-24)? And why would David's servants bring him a young virgin to try to resurrect David's ol' shriveled-up dick in his old age (I Kings 1:1-4)? Didn't Solomon have 700 wives and 300 concubines (I Kings 11:1-3)? Talk about a cum freak?! How about that fucker Ammon who raped his biological sister (II Sam. 13)? Remember Judah who fucked his daughter-in-law (Genesis 38)? And Absalom had sex with his daddy's concubines (II Sam. 16:21-22)!

If any of this shyt happened in our family today we would be outraged, but sadly, many of us would keep it as a "dirty little family secret." If what Latoya Jackson said is true, then, she's a brave soul for exposing ol' Joe's perversions! I personally know several women that have been sexually molested by their fathers but no one in the family wants to acknowledge the pain it's caused and confront the issue, especially the mothers of these bastards! And these poor women grow up thinking that somehow they are responsible for their father's perversions! (Read *Push*, by Sapphire)

This Bible that many hold so dear has taught us to *"honor thy father and mother"* at the expense of allowing our parents to physically and sexually abuse us! I'm enraged when I hear these sweet victims talk about trying to make amends with these child-molesting fathers before their father dies, when the fathers have not tried to ask forgiveness from their daughters first! Sistas! Fuck'em! Let them die and go straight to hell! I don't give a damn what your family says! You don't owe a fool like that no "last respects!" You oughta go down to the wake and spit on his rotting corpse! No, that shyt is not, "in the past!" No, don't just, "get over it!" The person who was supposed to protect you violated you! He killed your innocence! I'm talking about HETEROSEXUAL men!

The wives of these molesters are some of the most pathetic souls God has made. They stay with these men and justify their husband's perversion, which sends a signal to the child that it's their fault! There's so much freaky shyt goin' on in heterosexual's homes that it's a crying shame! And then many of these perverts show up Sunday to diss the homosexual and play "morality judge." Got the nerve to get up in the pulpit on a Sunday morning and preach "agape" (Christian love), only to go home and punch his wife in the face and stomp her to the ground in a parking lot! Give me a break! Nothing Prophetess Bynum could have said or done deserved what her ig-nant-assed preacher husband did to her! *W.W.J.D.* (What would Jesus do?) if he ran up on a scene like that? Like the moneychangers and dove sellers of 2,000 years ago who he chased out of the temple in a spiritual rage, Jesus would've stomped that nigga out for hitting a woman! Please believe dat!

Look at the statistics on marriage and divorce rates. Sixty percent divorce rate!? Oh, I see! Only heterosexuals should have the right to screw up, choose the wrong "soul mate," and then divorce! The so-called sanctity of marriage, for the most part, has become a big joke! As soon as we get the pussy or the dick, we're sprung! Talkin' 'bout I'm in love! No you ain't! You're in lust! A year later you're wondering who the fuck is in bed with you!

They want us to believe that heterosexual love is based on commitment and homosexual love is based on non-commitment and promiscuity. Look at these Hollywood marriages … You just know that it's only for a short appointed time. Michael Jackson and Lisa Marie? Who the hell do they think they were trying to fool? Michael wanted to "tap that ass" about as much as he wanted black skin, big lips, and a broad nose! Marriage and commitment just ain't what it used to be. The bottom line is that heterosexuals in this country have fucked up the institution of marriage, yet they want to form a united front to bar gays and lesbians from further fucking it up even more.

The biblical argument against homosexuality is a farce! They use neat little phrases like our "Judeo Christian Heritage is against homosexuality." Oh yeah, that's right! The same Judeo-Christian Heritage sanctified and justified slavery!? The same Judeo-Christian Heritage that allowed 20 million Africans to die for this white man's "Manifest Destiny!" The same Judeo-Christian Heritage that annihilated the Native Indians! Yeah, the same Judeo-Christian Heritage that segregated Blacks and marginalized women! I gotcha!

The phrase "Judeo-Christian Heritage" is a euphemism (nice language) for WHITE SUPREMACY because the traditions and heritage of this country didn't really change until a little over 30 years ago with the forced Civil Rights Movement. Before that it was the good ol' boy system of segregation and Jim Crowism and before that … slavery. Don't talk to me about Judeo-Christian values and shyt! Christianity is that box of cereal in the store marked "Cereal." You know the one … the generic brand! Without its pedigree with the Jews, as in "Judeo," it is empty.

Christians, if you really believe and insist that homosexuality is a crime against God, punishable by death, why don't you all enact some laws to that effect? If it's so damnable, why don't you good Christians kill a fag where you find one?! Drive them out of the land like King Asa! The Bible says they should be killed! But you're too chicken-shit to do that! All-of-a-sudden God's Word (the Bible), His/Her Law becomes too barbaric, primitive, savage, and uncivilized, right? That's too violent for your taste right? That should let you know that it's not God's Law, but primitive man's law dressed up in a holy robe! Those damned Levites who wrote down God's Law interjected and interpolated their own biases and prejudices about homosexuals just as they did about women and sex. Of all that is written in the Bible, homosexuality is a very, very minuscule part. Outside of the story of Sodom and Gomorrah, there isn't much said about them and in light of what I've just shown you about the Sodom story, we can exclude it also. There are FIVE scriptures in the Old Testament, which address the Sodomites but no one Sodomite is named or singled out for committing some heinous act like the heterosexuals in the Bible.

It's time to treat gays and lesbians as part of the human family. Abandon the homophobic teachings of the Christian church and recognize what's real. Homosexuality! Gay and lesbian hip-hop heads now have a formal response to homophobia within hip-hop. Please feel free to pass this book on to a brother or sister walking in homophobic darkness. The truth lives—now and forever!

"For all of your words of wisdom. For your bravery, acknowledgment and understanding. For the door you just helped to kick wide the fuck open. I am forever grateful. You just gave me more faith in myself and even MORE of a reason to stand up for myself, those like me and for the peace that does lie in human kind. Thank you for this piece and thank you for being, my brotha."

—*Much Love & Respect, Tori Fixx (Pioneering gay rap artist)*

Other books by Khalil Amani. (www.iuniverse.com, Barnes & Noble)

Khalilamani@yahoo.com www.myspace.com/khalilamani

Hard-core essays, relevant for a hip-hop generation.

Book Description

What up?! Just like to welcome you to this class here at W.F.U. I am Dr. Horatio Honeycutt. As you all know, a class in multicultural studies is required of all entering freshmen, so I'm happy that you've chosen this course to fulfill that requirement. I know that you will find this class stimulating, exciting, and truly challenging. So, welcome again!

I'm passing out a syllabus for your perusal. This semester you will get acquainted with Black people in the urban ghetto of this city. We will be going on a field-trip into the heart of the 'hood to get a firsthand look at how the language is spoken. But I must warn you, before we get to that point you must do a complete over-haul of your perception of Black people. We will have to become as "black" as we can be as not to standout and as they say in the hood, "get our asses bumrushed." In other words, we don't want to draw too much attention to ourselves and cause the indigenous population to pummel our bodies into mutilated pieces of DNA. But not to worry, I've already established communication with some of the more violent elements in the community. See?! You've already learned your first black word, "bumrush." It means to suddenly bombard without warning; to attack. Put it in your vocabulary, you'll need it.—Khalil Amani, Jive 101/Ebonics 1619

A hard-core, ghettorized summary on Judeo-Christian religion.

Book Description

Ghetto Religiosity 2000 is the first of a three-part series. It is the result of Mr. Amani's many years of study and disillusionment with organized religion. Often angry and filled with Ebonics and gangsta language, the author's quest is to reach those who have been removed from religion … those of us who have seen the church and the preacher manipulate the laity for their own selfish filthy lucre. If you're looking to read a watered-down "Jesus loves the world" text, this is not for you! This book is a hardcore, tellin'-it-like-it-is, new-jack, diatribe on the errors of Judeo-Christian Thought.

WHO SHALL MAKE IT PLAIN?
WHO SHALL TEACH THE YOUTH?
WHO SHALL SET THEM FREE?
—Khalil Amani, a religious gangsta

"A Ghettorized summary on the errors of Judeo-Christian Thought with relevant social commentary."

Book Description

Ghetto Religiosity II is the second of a three part series. The primary focus of this book is our religious understanding of sex. It is the author's premise that the sexual attitudes of today were erroneously and maliciously set up by men whose ultimate aim was to control the sexual practices of the ancient Jews and the rights of women. The author explores the mythology behind the "Fall of Man" in the Garden of Eden and how that story has denigrated women. Most controversial is our present view of homosexuality and how the Bible has thoroughly misshaped our ideas about homosexual love. The case is made that homosexuality is not a sin against God but rather a conspiracy conjured up by the machinations of the ancient Levitical priests to keep the Israelites from engaging in Goddess religions and the Sodomite cult.

A hard-core analysis of religion through the eyes of a hip hop head

Book Description

Khalil Amani has done it again! With his third installment of the *Ghetto Religiosity* series, Amani brings it home like fish & grits! He has done to religion what your mama does in the kitchen—Put his foot all up in it!

Of great interest is Amani's critique and analysis of his former teacher, Yahweh Ben Yahweh. Amani cogently deconstructs Yahweh theology with the precision of a neurosurgeon, giving us a detailed account of Yahweh teachings, which have been exposed as plagiarisms from the Nation of Islam among others.

Perhaps most controversial is Amani's scathing and blistering attack on 9/11 and our religious and secular perceptions/ideas about why this tragedy occurred. Amani takes exception to and rejects the pseudo-religiosity of 9/11. In his usual hard-core fashion, Amani puts God's business on front-street and asks the critical questions about God's whereabouts in our time of need. This book is not for the faint of heart!

Truths Hurt

A memoir detailing the life of a religious cult member and his involvement in the Witness Protection Program.

Book Description

At the age of twenty, Khalil Amani joined a Black Hebrew Israelite sect in Miami, Florida. For five years he endured hell on earth-witnessing and having information about beatings, welfare scams, and murders.

Left spiritually devastated, Khalil left the sect, living a very dysfunctional life—a decadent and promiscuous life—womanizing, drug dealing, exotic dancing—a life filled with lustful tales and shadowy characters—ever shaping his world.

Khalil became the outspoken critic and number one disgruntled ex-member, recounting on TV and in the newspapers the horrors and atrocities committed by the Yahweh sect.

After a trial, in which he was the first of 160 witnesses testifying against Yahweh ben Yahweh, Khalil entered the Federal Witness Security Program, where he gives us a detailed account of the inner-workings of the Program—from someone who's actually been accepted into the government's ultra-secretive identity make-over machine. This is one black man's harrowing tale of survival in urban America—a brutally honest introspection on self, family, sex, race, religion. In the end ... there is redemption for all!

—"The bravest man I know!"

Sydney P. Freedberg—Pulitzer Prize Journalist and Author of *Brother Love: Murder, Money, and a Messiah.*

Works Cited

Amani, Khalil. *Ghetto Religiosity 2000: Third Millennium Liberation.* Lincoln: Iuniverse.com, 2000.

Amani, Khalil. *Ghetto Religiosity II: Uncovering The Naked Truth.* Lincoln: Iuniverse.com, 2001.

American Psychiatric Association. *Stance On Homosexuality.*

Applegate, Kenneth. *Voltaire On Religion: Selected Writings.* New York: Frederick Ungar Publishing, 1974.

Barnstone, Willis. *The Other Gospel.* New York:
The Gospel of Philip, The Secret Gospel of Mark.
HarperSan Francisco, 1984.

Beasley, James R., et al. *An Introduction To The Bible.* Nashville: Abingdon Press, 1991.

Berube, Margery S., et al. *The American Heritage Dictionary.* Boston: Houghton Mifflin Company, 1982.

Buttrick, George A. *The Interpreter's Dictionary of the Bible.* Vols. E-J, K-Q. New York: Abingdon Press, 1962.

Crim, Keith et al. *The Interpreter's Dictionary of the Bible.* (Supplementary Volume). Nashville: Parthenon Press, 1976.

Eilberg-Schwartz, Howard. *God's Phallus and Other Problems for Men and Monotheism.* Boston: Beacon Press, 1994.

Holy Bible. King James Version. Masonic ed. Chicago:
John Hertel Co., 1957.

Jones, James H. *Bad Blood: The Tuskegee Syphilis Experiment.* New York: The Free Press, 1993.

Kaufmann, Walter. *The Portable Nietzsche.* New York.
     Penguin Press, 1954.

Kugel, James L. *The Bible As It Was.* Cambridge, Mass.:
     The Belknap Press of Harvard University Press, 1997.

Mack, Burton L. *Who Wrote The New Testament: The Making of the Christian Myth.* San Francisco: HarperSan Francisco, 1995.

Metzger, Bruce M. and Michael D. Coogan. *The Oxford Companion to the Bible.* New York: Oxford University Press, 1993.

Myers, Allen C. *The Eerdmans Bible Dictionary.* Grand Rapids:
     William B. Eerdmans Publishing Co., 1987.

Rathus, Spencer A. et al. *Psychology.* 4th Ed. Ft. Worth:
     Holt, Rhinehart, and Winston, 1996.

Russell, Paul. *The Gay 100.* Caral Publishing Group, 1995.

Selassie, Haile. *Selected Speeches.*

Stone, Merlin. *When God Was A Woman.* San Diego:
     Harcourt Brace & Co., 1976.

Sunderland, J.T. *The Origin and Character of the Bible.* Boston:
     American Unitarian Association, 1908.

World Bible Publishers. *The Holy Bible.* (King James Version).

Selected Lyrics

Deadlee. *Assault With A Deadlee Weapon.* 2005. (Bombastic records)
DJ Quik. *Quik Is The Name.* 1991. (Arista/Profile)
Dr. Dre. *The Chronic.* 1992. (Aftermath)
Canibus. *Can-I-Bus.* 1998. (Universal)
Common. *Electric Circus.* 2002. (MCA Records)
Elephant Man. *A Nuh Fi Wi Fault.* 1999. (Bad Man Remix)
Eminem. *The Marshall Mathers LP.* 2000. (Aftermath)
FELONi. *A Woman's Revenge.* 2007. (Trak Diamond Records)
50 Cent. *Get Rich Or Die Tryin'.* 2003. (Shady/Aftermath)
Grandmaster Flash. *The Message.* 1982. (Sugar Hill Records)
Jay-Z. *The Black Album.* 2003. (Roc-A-Fella)
LL Cool J. *Mama Said Knock You Out.* 1990. (Def Jam)
MC Lyte *Ain't No Other.* 1993. (First Priority)
Rick Ross. *Port Of Miami.* 2006. (Slip-N-Slide/Rock-A-Fella)

978-0-595-47541-4
0-595-47541-8